Survival in Russia

CHAOS AND HOPE
IN EVERYDAY LIFE

Lois Fisher

WESTVIEW PRESS

Boulder • San Francisco • Oxford

English edition copyright © 1993 by Westview Press, Inc.

English edition published in 1993 in the United States of America by Westview Press, Inc., 5500 Central Avenue, Boulder, Colorado 80301-2877, and in the United Kingdom by Westview Press, 36 Lonsdale Road, Summertown, Oxford OX2 7EW

German edition copyright © 1991 by Hoffmann und Campe Verlag, Hamburg

German edition published in 1991 as *Überleben in Rußland: Chaos und Hoffnung im Alltag* by Hoffmann und Campe Verlag, Hamburg

Library of Congress Cataloging-in-Publication Data
Fisher, Lois, 1940–
    [Überleben in Russland: Chaos und Hoffnung im Alltag. English]
    Survival in Russia: chaos and hope in everyday life / Lois
Fisher.
        p.   cm.
    ISBN 0-8133-8629-2—ISBN 0-8133-8630-6 (pbk.)
    1. Soviet Union—Social life and customs—1970–1991.   2. Soviet
Union—Description and travel—1970–1991.   3. Fisher-Ruge, Lois,
1940–   —Journeys—Soviet Union.   I. Title.
DK287.F5713   1993
947.085'4—dc20   92-44177
                                                                            CIP

Printed and bound in the United States of America

The paper used in this publication meets the requirements
of the American National Standard for Permanence of Paper
for Printed Library Materials Z39.48-1984.

10   9   8   7   6   5   4   3   2   1

For Wolf, the first reader of this book

Contents

vii

INTRODUCTION

THE WEEPING VOICE of my Russian friend Marcia jarred me out of sleep at my apartment in Cologne. It was 6 A.M. on August 19, 1991, and she told me about the Kremlin coup. She had just phoned her husband in Moscow, who cautioned her not to return home, as she had planned that day.

She was on holiday with her son in Israel and asked me what she should do. I also advised her to stay put until the situation was clearer. During the next two days I was in frequent contact with Marcia, but I could not reach my other friends in Russia. I worried that their lives might be endangered and felt helpless and desperate.

Moscow was the last place in the world where I wanted to live when we moved there in 1977, but I did not have much choice. My former husband, a German journalist, considered hardship posts an irresistible challenge, and so we packed our bags once again for a new assignment. I had just spent four lonely and hard years in Beijing at the end of the Cultural Revolution and was looking forward to settling down in the "decadent" West, but that wish had to be postponed for another four years.

While adjusting to the Moscow way of life, I was often reminded of Beijing. We were once again assigned an apartment in a foreign compound, with guards at the gate, who stopped and even humiliated Russian guests. A visit to other parts of the country required permission from the Foreign Ministry. The foreigners had their own special shops, where they could buy what the Russians could not buy. The Soviet media discouraged contact with foreigners. We might be spies, they warned. In spite of this anti-Western propaganda I made friends who opened their doors and hearts to me.

Natasha was my first friend. She was standing behind me in a bread line when other customers started shouting at me. I did not understand a

3

word, and she came to my rescue. The sleeve of my coat was touching loaves of bread, she explained in English, and people thought it was un-sanitary. This meeting led to many more, and eventually she introduced me to her circle of friends. I had passed the "trust" test and had a key to the world around me.

I could not find work in Moscow, so the day belonged to me and to the Russians. Just when I was beginning to speak Russian with ease and confidence and to feel at home we were transferred to Cologne, Germany.

I did not want to leave Moscow, which made my adjustment to life in the West more difficult. I missed the warmth and compassion of my Moscow friends and found every excuse to return as often as possible. I began writing about these people and this activity brought us even closer.

In the mid-1980s after Gorbachev came to power the atmosphere in Moscow changed decisively. My friends were no longer careful about where they met me or what they said. They could visit me in Cologne, read the literature they chose, and openly criticize the system. They felt as though the doors of prison had been opened. Through their encourage-ment, I decided to return to Moscow as a journalist. I received an accredi-tation for a German magazine that allowed me to have a work visa and a flat in the center of Moscow. Now I commute monthly between my apart-ment in Cologne and my apartment in Moscow. This book is a product of many of those trips.

The sensational victory of the democratic forces in August 1991 brought me enormous relief and joy. The defeat of the conservative forces, which had opposed reforms, meant that the democratic process might be accelerated. But it did not mean that the hardships of everyday life would be swept aside overnight and that the mentality of people would be changed at once. It will be many years before the situations that I describe in this book improve perceptibly.

This book has turned out to be more critical and political than my other books about the Soviet Union due to the rapidly changing times. In *Alltag in Moskau* (Everyday life in Moscow), which I wrote in the early

1980s, I described the life of my Russian friends, while carefully avoiding politics. During that period, Russians who had unofficial contact with foreigners risked interrogation by the KGB and even imprisonment.

Nadezhda Means Hope emerged from my euphoria about Gorbachev's commitment to glasnost, perestroika, democracy, and a freer society. In *Meine armenischen Kinder* (My Armenian children) my role had changed from an observer to a participant, and I described the Soviet system as I experienced it, from the inside. I was appalled by the ghastly medical conditions and reacted by organizing German medical assistance for young victims of the Armenian earthquake in 1988.

Since early 1990 I shared the outlook of my Russian friends, who wavered between complete despair and glimmering hope for a country that is in the stage of a dramatic upheaval. In summer 1990 I noticed a radical deterioration in living conditions in Moscow. The shops were empty. Drugstores did not even have aspirin. No one wanted to work hard and crime was on the rise. Only those with foreign currency had no worries. They belong to the small privileged group I call "first class" Soviet citizens. They could and still can afford to pay for the "deficit items"—scarce items—the ruble cannot buy.

Everyone from students to pensioners talked about the failures of Gorbachev's perestroika, without recognizing that its success was also dependent on their participation. The majority of Muscovites opposed the Communist party as the leading power. Many even joined the reformers, who advocated a multiparty system, private property, and a market economy.

In my other books I purposely avoided discussing politics, but now it is impossible to be apolitical when writing about the current Russian world. No one can dispute the fact that Gorbachev initiated a revolution that changed the image of the Soviet Union abroad. At the same time he set into motion a series of unplanned events at home that overwhelmed him. Violent confrontations among members of different nationalities; the political disintegration of the Union; miners' strikes; anti-Gorbachev demonstrations; catastrophic food and consumer shortages; the flagrant neglect of the victims of Chernobyl; and bloodbaths in Baku, Tbilisi, and the Baltic republics destabilized the country and diminished Gorbachev's power, popularity, and credibility at home.

I regard Gorbachev as a tragic figure and feel sympathy for him. The emergence of Yeltsin and other reformers has given me renewed hope. When the democratic process is deeply rooted in the former Soviet Union, pioneers for perestroika will no longer be exceptions, like those in my book, who are struggling for their rights as human beings. They will be examples for the future.

I have written about the lives and attitudes of people whose government neglected, exploited, and humiliated them for more than seventy-four years. Each person in this book has found a way to survive during these difficult times and still retains hope for a better future.

The harshness of life and the injustices of the system will shock some readers. But this reality may help them to understand why it will take decades before the mentality of people will change and Russians will be able to lead a life with honor and dignity.

1

MY FRIEND,
THE BLACK MARKETEER

KIRIL'S PARENTS wanted their only son to be a diplomat. But, instead, he decided to be a black marketeer. I first met Kiril in June 1990, when he was sixteen years old. He was standing with a group of other teenage boys in front of the Beriozka shop around the corner from my Moscow flat. I passed this store where only foreign currency can be used to buy Russian goods and imported items daily on my way to the bus stop and assumed these boys were foreign tourists. One was wearing the latest Western fashion—baggy Bermuda shorts in gaudy colors that began at his knees and reached a crescendo of bad taste with his clashing shirt.

Another, who turned out to be Kiril, was more conservatively dressed in a black Batman T-shirt, sneakers, and faded jeans fashionably shredded at the knees. His short brown hair, tall slim build, and open friendly face made him look like a typical American. My prolonged stare at his comically dressed friend gave Kiril the wrong signal. "Do you want to buy something?" he asked, in an English that had a slight southern drawl.

I felt foolish for misjudging the situation but replied, "What are you selling?" He unzipped his shoulder bag and let me peer inside. Apparently he did not want to display his wares openly in such a public place. The jar of caviar cost $15, which was a bargain. In the Beriozka shop it was at least five times more expensive. The military watch, which was popular among tourists at that time, cost $20, and the finely painted, lacquered box with miniature scenes—a product of the famous Palekh factory—was selling for $50.

The price of the caviar was tempting, but I refused. It was illegal for a foreigner to buy anything on the black market, and I abided by this law. If the authorities wanted to find fault with my conduct, then it should be for a better reason. This was my first contact with a black marketeer, and I was curious about his profession. I also wanted to know why such an intelligent-looking young man was involved in work that could land him in prison any day.

To be fair to Kiril, I told him at once that I was a journalist and that I had no intention of doing business with him. I simply wanted to talk to him about his work, providing it would not get him into trouble. At that moment I assumed, without being paranoid, that we were probably being observed by KGB agents. He laughed at my concern. He was afraid of plainclothesmen, not of foreign journalists.

It was a warm, sunny day, and we made an appointment to meet an hour later while the store was closed for lunch. We found a rickety park bench nearby in green, quiet surroundings. Kiril sat silently, waiting for me to begin. His swinging left leg crossed over his right knee showed his nervousness. To put him at ease I chatted about myself and my family. He was particularly interested in the lives of teenagers in the United States. When his left leg finally stopped swinging, I began asking questions and he answered willingly.

Kiril preferred to speak English, but when he could not think of a word, he switched to Russian. He had learned English in a "special" school, where English instruction began in the second, and not the fourth grade, which was the case in most schools. This school was also "special" because the majority of its pupils were children of high party functionaries, well-known artists, and scientists. Kiril was an exception. His father, a night watchman, and his mother, a cleaning woman, believed their son had the right to a good education. Kiril passed the school's entrance exam, which gave him access to an exclusive Moscow world.

For the first seven grades Kiril was an exemplary pupil. His high marks in English and his good behavior made him the favorite of his English teacher, who occasionally invited him and his mother to her home. He also excelled in sports, but these distinctions did not help him to overcome his feeling of inferiority.

When pupils collected old paper for the school, Kiril had the opportunity to see how his rich classmates lived. Their homes were in well-kept apartment buildings where neither litter nor unpleasant smells filled the stairwells, as was the case in his neighborhood. The buildings had pensioners as concierges, who sat in glassed-in areas in the entrance halls to observe those who were coming and going. The pensioners knew the faces of all of the residents and greeted Kiril's classmates; he felt proud when they also smiled at him.

At first he was impressed by the same "funny" wallpaper in each apartment. "The walls looked like a photograph," he said. Only the landscapes and scenes differed from home to home. I had seen this kind of photo-wallpaper in the pompously furnished flat of a friend who belonged to the *nomenklatura* —the privileged Communist establishment. The walls of her living room projected a three-dimensional look, like some screens in movie theaters, and I felt as though I were sitting in the middle of the woods.

After this brief exposure to the world of the rich and privileged, Kiril had many other opportunities to compare his living standards with theirs. "When I was in the homes of my classmates, I noticed for the first time how poor we were and knew I could never invite them to my home. They had VCRs and color televisions. All of their furniture was imported. They ate delicacies that I had never seen in our shops."

When Kiril recalled painful experiences from his childhood his dark brown eyes lost their twinkle and he started fidgeting with the thin gold ring in his left earlobe. "My classmates always wore the latest Western fashions that my parents could not afford. They arrived at discotheques in their 'washed out' jeans, and I looked like a village bumpkin in my Russian-made clothes. I felt ashamed and uncomfortable when we were together."

While Kiril spoke, I was reminded of the Russian proverb that I had first heard when I came to the Soviet Union in 1977, "You judge a person first by his clothing and later by his intelligence." Clothing gives young people status, prestige, and self-confidence, and some parents, I knew, had three jobs so that their children could be dressed in imported clothes.

In 1989, at the age of fifteen, Kiril worked in a cooperative—private business—selling beer during his summer holiday and earned 600 rubles a month, at a time when the average salary was 200 rubles. This was much more than his parents brought home together, but he still was not satisfied. "I worked a twelve-hour shift, doing the work of three people and received a salary for only one." Exhausted and embittered, he quit, vowing that he would be his own boss in the future.

That summer job changed the course of Kiril's life. For the first time he had money in his pocket for expensive Western clothing, and he wanted to earn more. Kiril lost interest in his studies that fall and skipped school. He did not come home every night, but met new friends in a park in his working-class neighborhood where they played the guitar, smoked, and dreamed of being rich one day.

Teachers threatened his parents that he would have to repeat a grade. The next summer Kiril crammed to make up for his truancy and received top grades again. In January 1991, one semester before he was supposed to graduate, he left school. "I knew that I did not have the same chances as many of my classmates. I would have liked to have been a diplomat or an interpreter, which was the wish of my parents, but these professions required connections. My parents were only simple workers and knew no one with influence. At best, I could be an engineer, but the profession is so poorly paid that my life would have been an endless struggle. If one wants to live well in this country education is not necessary," Kiril said.

His first contact with black marketeers had been in 1989 after he had earned money for expensive Western goods that summer. He met them in front of the Hotel Rossiya, which is located between Red Square and the Moscow River. One of his working-class friends had passed the hotel and, seeing a foreigner, asked for a cigarette. The foreigner gave him a whole pack. Kiril and his best friend, Sasha, tried the same ploy and had even better luck: They received two packs.

From that day on Kiril hung around the Rossiya and met other kinds of black marketeers who did business with foreign guests. He learned that the "small fry," who were fourteen and younger, made a business of exchanging Lenin badges for cigarettes and gum. Older teenagers, who wore expensive Levi's and name-brand sneakers, were selling military hats; this sight inspired Kiril to begin business.

When Sasha found a military hat at home, he and Kiril went to the Hotel Cosmos, another hotel for foreigners, the next day and an Englishman gave them £7 for the hat. With their first foreign earnings in hand, they went to another type of black marketeer, one whose business was to exchange foreign currency for rubles. He gave them 40 rubles, which he said was the black-market price at that time. Had Sasha and Kiril been experienced they would have known that the hat was selling for £12 and they could have earned 90 rubles elsewhere.

Kiril learned the ropes quickly and in a short time made connections with people who sold him products that foreigners wanted to buy. He met a man who worked in the factory where military watches were produced and began doing business with him. He also traveled to a small village near Moscow to visit an artist who would supply him lacquered boxes, like the one he had shown me when we first met.

This business was not without risk. In 1986, when cooperatives were officially permitted, the word "racketeer" entered the Russian vocabulary. Racketeers demand "protection money" from those who engage in the private business sector, such as cooperative owners, joint venture firms, and even street sellers like Kiril. If the racketeers are not paid, they can be dangerous. In some cases they have burned down cooperatives and killed their owners. A Soviet journalist who filmed a documentary on racketeers was found strangled in her car.

Kiril, who was only a "small fry," had to pay a monthly fee of 300 rubles to a racketeer, so that he could work in peace in front of my neighborhood Beriozka shop. In April 1991, when prices rose in the country, Kiril's racketeer increased the monthly payment to 500 rubles. If Kiril refused, he said, "They could strip me of my expensive clothing and even beat me up." The only time racketeers are useful as "protectors" is against other gangsters who might rob their "customer." The racketeer's job is to find the robber and return the money, for an additional fee, of course. Kiril's racketeer visited him weekly to make certain that everything was in order. He belonged to one of the notorious groups of racketeers, who are known by the name of the town they come from. These men, in their twenties, belong to the working class and prepare for their job by bodybuilding. I had seen such types strutting around Moscow and never would have wanted to be muscled by them.

The racketeer could protect Kiril from robbers, but not from being taken into police custody. His first confrontation with legal authorities was in 1990 shortly after he had begun selling military hats. A plain-clothesman saw a transaction and took him to a police station, where he had to relinquish his $5. If Kiril had had more than $40 in foreign currency with him, it would have been an offense punishable by imprisonment. This was a lesson for the future: He had to avoid being caught with foreign currency. The second time he was taken into custody he learned from others that the police can be bribed, and soon he was free.

The third time the police informed his parents, who were shocked to learn of their son's illegal activities. His mother's tears and disappointment moved him to make a promise he could not keep. He would quit black marketeering, but that lasted only for a few weeks. "I had the feeling of money and its power, and became its captive," he said.

Kiril's business was a forbidden subject at home, and his parents asked him not to flaunt his earnings. He was now financially independent and could afford to spend money on items that made their lives a little more comfortable. He bought, from time to time, meat for 25 rubles a kilo at the private market and clothing for his sister Katya at black-market prices. The real luxury was a VCR, which thrilled the entire family. It also came in handy to me because I did not have a VCR in Moscow.

In the fall of 1990, after I had gotten to know Kiril, I wanted to show him a video of the film *We Cannot Live Like This*—a documentary that had been acclaimed at film festivals abroad and was the topic of heated discussion among my Soviet friends. Crime in the Soviet Union was its main theme. Since the end of the 1980s the crime rate in the Soviet Union had increased considerably, which was shocking to Soviet citizens. At the same time it was far lower than in Europe and the United States.

One film critic called the documentary "merciless." Another, who was a member of the Soviet parliament, said, "If this film were shown all over the country, major changes would take place in the ruling party. Such a film helps people to overcome fear of the authorities."

Kiril had heard about the film and was as eager as I to see it. I was also interested in his reaction and hoped, at the same time, I would have the opportunity to meet his family. We agreed to meet in front of the Beriozka shop after his workday, which began at 11:00 A.M. and ended at 7:00 P.M.

He greeted me with his usual smile and then flagged down a taxi. After Kiril gave the driver the address and flashed a 10-ruble bill in front of his nose he was willing to take us. In the past the meter in the taxi determined the price. Now taxi drivers tell passengers how much the ride will cost before they enter the taxi, and this is usually at least four times more than the meter rate. If the driver hears a foreign accent, he demands dollars.

The run-down condition of Kiril's apartment house was typical for most Moscow buildings. The staircase was missing chunks of cement, and wires and rusty pipes were exposed. The missing light bulbs, due to one of Moscow's infinite shortages, made the walk up to the fourth floor treacherous.

A purring ball of mischief greeted us and ran along playfully while Kiril gave me a quick tour of the three-room flat. "Formerly we had to share this space with three other families," he said. "After two of the families moved out three years ago Katya was born, and we were permitted to keep the flat for ourselves." The official living norm, I knew, permits each person a 12-square-meter [129-square-foot] living area.

This flat was a paradise compared to the family's former living quarters, Kiril told me. His father came to Moscow from Siberia and his mother from Belorussia as *limitchiki,* more than twenty years ago. Limitchiki are people from other cities who are given special permission to live in Moscow because they perform the menial jobs that Muscovites do not fill. After a certain number of workyears they earn the right to remain in the capital and to move out of squalid, overcrowded living quarters into apartments. Kiril's father gave up guitar playing to sweep Moscow's streets. His mother became a cleaning woman, although she had studied to be a draftsman.

Their first living space was a dark, cold cellar with no plumbing. The nearest public toilet was in a museum, a ten-minute bus ride away. The second flat had a room with a toilet, but no heating or hot water. The third had a kitchen, where Kiril remembers eating on top of a suitcase placed on a broken chair. They had been living in their present apartment for eight years, but they felt at home only after the other two families moved out.

The VCR and television were in Kiril's room, where his neatness shamed me in comparison to my apartment. His desktop was almost clear, and the English and Russian books in the hanging bookshelves stood neatly in rows. Not a fingerprint was visible on the lacquered wooden doors of his closet. The burgundy carpet hanging on the wall gave the room a touch of color. I settled into a comfortable, worn chair, and Kiril sat in the middle of his sofa bed to watch the film, which we had heard so much about. "When my mother returns from kindergarten with Katya, she will prepare tea and a bite to eat," he said.

When film director Stanislav (Slava) Govorukhin appeared on the screen in the first scene, in the role of a journalist, I remembered a conversation we had three years before, in 1987, when he lived in Odessa. He told me then, "I have given up my profession as a journalist in this country to become a director because as a journalist I would have to lie." At that time he was best known for the film he made with his now-deceased friend Vladimir Vysotsky, an actor and singer whose songs about life touched the hearts of the nation. Young people remembered Govorukhin for his Agatha Christie and Tom Sawyer films.

The era of glasnost finally permitted the then fifty-four-year-old director to air his political views. One of my friends had studied with Slava at the film institute many years ago and described him as "the only free and independent person I know. He has always been a fighter for what he believes in and courageously defends the truth and points out the lies, even when it costs him friendships." The film, which we were seeing at that moment, verified her remarks.

The journalist Govorukhin began with an introductory statement: "In our film we are not showing spectacular trials and complicated crimes. The criminality that you will see is not unusual ... but that does not mean that it is less shocking. It concerns everyone. The reasons are profound and should be taken seriously."

After this remark I was not prepared for the shocking crime scenes that followed: murdered men stretched out on the ground, the naked bodies of young girls who had been abused and disfigured, a giggling mother who had starved her two babies to death. Six teenage boys on trial for the rape and murder of a classmate joked in front of the camera, and not one showed remorse. A Russian Orthodox priest commented: "The increasing brutality frightens and worries me. It is a national tragedy. The reason is the loss of values, a loss of human feelings. God has been done away with."

While Kiril sat immobile and speechless as one harsh scene led to the next, I recalled my conversation only a few weeks before with Slava and his wife, Galya, in their Moscow apartment. I had not seen him in four years, and he looked beaten and exhausted. The wrinkles on his forehead extended to his bald head. His eyes were tired and his face unsmiling. While smoking one cigarette after another he spoke so quietly that I had to strain to understand him.

"The greatest crime of the government during the last seventy years was to create a new kind of person," he said, "a person without moral values. People have stopped working, and chaos and anarchy reign. Everything is leading to the country's rapid decline. The situation is similar to the time of the 1917 revolution when people were striking and did not want to work for the party. Lenin's solution was to execute the saboteurs, black marketeers, priests, those who complained about criminality. Through this method the people were forced to work again. They were slaves."

Slava continued this theme. "People who are accustomed to live as slaves should not be given freedom at once. Democracy is a slow, long-term process. You have noticed that the freedom we have won has side effects, such as lawlessness, immorality, envy, aggressiveness."

In 1987 I had believed that democracy and perestroika would rescue the country from collapse. My friends had even encouraged me to write

Nadezhda Means Hope. Now it is difficult to find anyone with more than a drop of hope. "You wrote your work during a romantic period when we were euphoric after our first breath of freedom and now everything looks different," a journalist said.

Was perestroika a mistake? I asked Galya, who finally had time to sit down with us after serving a delicious multicourse meal. In a quiet voice she said that she did not like to talk about politics and then began, "Perestroika freed Slava. The lies with which he had to live no longer burden his soul. He can now say what he wants."

Galya had not exaggerated. Not only were the scenes of Govorukhin's film shocking, but the boldness of his script amazed me. While I sat there not believing my ears, Kiril nodded his head.

While children played in the foreground at a Pioneer camp where they were spending their summer holiday, I heard the film director's words, "This is the laboratory of the animal breeders." While they sang a patriotic song, he said, "In no country of the world is the psyche of the children destroyed to such an extent." Govorukhin patted a statue of Lenin somewhere on the grounds of the Pioneer camp and said, "We have gotten rid of one God and replaced him with another."

The camera focused on an imposing building in Kiev, which turned out to be the Lenin museum. The director's comment: "Does the government despise its people so much that instead of building schools, hospitals, and living quarters, it spends millions of rubles on a museum in honor of a man who was never in Kiev?"

In a city in Siberia, Govorukhin showed a seemingly unending line for vodka on a Friday afternoon. Veterans and invalids were permitted to go to the head of the queue, and the director remarked ironically, "How touching! They did not fight in vain. The government did not forget their services to their country." In the background a male voice from the queue shouted, "They have left us nothing except vodka." The director agreed. "For years they filled people with vodka, so they would forget their suffering and problems, and no longer see, hear, or think."

The final scene was the tearing down of the Berlin Wall. Govorukhin asked the question that I had so often asked. "Why did they build this wall? What did they have to defend: poverty against wealth and suppression against freedom?"

When the film ended, Kiril and I sat in silence. Then he said, "It was a sad film, but everything is true." At that moment I heard the front door open and within seconds Kiril's mother and sister entered the room. His mother was surprised to find a guest in her apartment. I had asked Kiril not to mention my visit, because I wanted to avoid the elaborate preparations that characterize Russian hospitality. I also knew that my presence would create great excitement.

Kiril introduced me to his mother, Liuda, who said in a cheerful voice, "You are the first foreign guest in our apartment, and, what is more, an American. I am delighted to meet you." It was late, but she insisted that I drink a hot cup of tea with bread and homemade marmalade before she put Katya to bed.

The atmosphere was relaxed and I did not feel for a second like a stranger. Kiril told his mother about the film we had just seen, and Liuda asked if she and her husband could see it. I agreed to leave the film with them and pick it up at a later date.

When Kiril helped me into my coat and insisted on accompanying me home in the taxi, I regarded this as something special. Western emancipation had made me almost forget that gallant gentlemen still exist. "On the way home, I will visit my girlfriend," he shouted to his mother through the almost closed door, and Liuda responded like most mothers. "Don't be too late," she called after him.

A few weeks later Liuda called to invite me to visit them, and Kiril and I arrived a few minutes before his mother. When Liuda entered the apartment she looked like a million dollars. She wore a beige suede coat with a fur border and a matching voluminous fur hat. Under her coat was a brown, shapeless knit skirt and sweater. Like most Russian women, she had invested all of her savings in a luxurious facade.

This time I noticed how pretty Liuda was, with big blue eyes and a smile that warmed up the room. Her flawless skin, rosy cheeks, and sparkling white teeth made her look younger than her forty-three years.

She ushered us into the kitchen and set the table with bread, home-made marmalades—which she fetched from behind the curtains in Kiril's room—boiled potatoes, and, to my amazement, even butter. This was a time when butter was not available in shops and cost 50 rubles a kilo at private markets.

I was relieved that the table was not sagging with numerous dishes, which are just as much a part of Russian hospitality as the overfed guest, but this was a reflection of the times. Only those with money or connections could afford to eat sausage and cheese, formerly staples, even for the working class.

Liuda admitted that she was better off than many other mothers. A few years before she had become a cook in a kindergarten in order to secure a place in the school for Katya. Otherwise, Katya couldn't have entered the overcrowded kindergarten. Liuda was responsible for cooking for seventy children and the staff. Familiar with the food problems of mothers I asked if the school was affected by shortages. "We don't have pineapples and other rarities," she said laughing, "but we have the essentials, such as meat and potatoes."

Her salary, including overtime, was only 180 rubles a month, but Liuda's job gave her what money could not buy. "When I work in the evening, and some parents pick up their children before dinner, portions are uneaten. Instead of throwing the food away, I bring home the leftovers, but I would never bring home a whole fish," she reassured me. She did not have to convince me of her integrity. It was written on her face.

Four-year-old Katya was accustomed to being the center of attention like most Russian children, and when she started acting up, Kiril took her out of the kitchen to distract her. This gave Liuda the chance to speak openly. "The money Kiril earns is not honest. I don't want to see it or hear about it." "But it makes your life easier," I said. "It's true, but he knows that I am against him bringing home anything for us that he has bought with that money. The exception is a birthday. Last year he gave me my first bottle of French perfume and Katya warm winter shoes. Only once did I ask him for 50 rubles. That was when my wallet was stolen."

Kiril had overheard a part of the conversation and returned to the kitchen to defend himself. I was used to his good-natured, quiet manner, but he was now on home territory and had the right to raise his voice. "If a person works and lives honestly here, he can barely exist on his salary. Those who have money are considered criminals, but it is impossible to earn money honestly. I am not a criminal. I have not stolen from anyone or forced anyone to buy anything from me. I have only offered to sell what I bought," he said.

Liuda interrupted him and spoke even louder, "Based on our laws, you are a criminal. The judge may sympathize with you, but he must make a decision based on the laws." Lowering her voice, she said, "I am afraid of a bad end for Kiril. I can't sleep peacefully. I have tried to pray, but I don't really know how, and it wouldn't help anyway. Money alone cannot bring happiness. When Kiril was young we were very poor, but we were happy. He was a friendly child with a kind disposition. I remember the day when Kiril joined the young Pioneer organization. He was so excited that he could not speak. He believed in something then, but today he is like many other young people. He believes in nothing. Each person must try to preserve human values and live morally."

Kiril was annoyed at his mother's preaching and said, "Business is my interest and since it is not legal here I will go to America where capitalism is allowed." "What will you do in America?" Liuda asked in amazement. "You won't find any work." "Don't believe everything you read in Soviet newspapers about unemployment in the West," Kiril said. "Look at Lois, she is a journalist and has qualifications." "What can you offer?" Liuda asked. "At the beginning I will find work where no skills are required. I don't want to be president. Every day I live in fear because I don't know what tomorrow will bring," he said.

Liuda apologized for conducting a heated discussion in my presence and switched to a theme that included me. "Katya's first words when she entered her class were, 'Tonight we have an American guest.' A foreigner, particularly an American, is highly respected here." "I have experienced this often," I said. Liuda continued, "It's best to be a foreigner here. Then you are treated like a human being, not like a piece of paper."

The veneration for foreigners dates back to Peter the Great, a friend told me. When Peter wanted to reward a loyal employee with a special distinction he first offered him money and then medals. Refusing both, the employee asked to be called a foreigner in Russia.

"We have national pride here, but we know that your life is easier and better in many ways," Liuda said. I interrupted to repeat what I had so often said to friends, "I feel badly that I am treated like a first-class person in your country, only because of foreign currency, while Soviet citizens are subject to one humiliation after another. I have the privileges and possibilities that are denied to you."

Volodia, Kiril's father, entered at that moment and somehow I was surprised by his appearance. I don't know what I expected, but certainly not a man who looked like a philosopher. He was slight and had a full, salt-and-pepper colored beard that was evenly trimmed. He greeted me shyly and then took Katya away to wash her chocolate-covered face and hands.

While we had been waiting for Volodia to come home, Liuda had spoken affectionately about him. When Katya was sick, he had taken a part-time job in order to take care of her. At that time Liuda did not want to give up her steady employment, which was the main support for the family. Now he worked in a kindergarten as an electrician. He loved reading and playing the guitar, and if he had been able to choose his profession, he would have been a musician. In the past he had been interested in politics and had great faith in Gorbachev. After soldiers mowed down innocent people in the Baltic republics he no longer trusted him. Now he found peace in ethereal matters. He was not alone. Many of my friends considered the events in the Soviet Union so irrational that they said, half jokingly, that they were living in the theater of the absurd. And so they sought comfort in astrology, the supernatural, and religion.

When Kiril's father returned to the kitchen, Liuda left with Katya, so that she would not interrupt our conversation again. In contrast to his daughter, who was loud and full of enthusiasm, Volodia spoke in a whisper. While searching for words he paused pensively, as though afraid that he might say the wrong thing. I listened attentively, trying to understand subjects that were far-out for me, such as UFOs, astrological matters, and signals from outer space.

The one time he showed emotion was when he talked about the government's neglect of the Chernobyl victims, especially the estimated 800,000 children, who should have been evacuated and treated immediately after that tragedy in April 1986. "That was a greater disaster than the catastrophe itself," he said. "Chernobyl is like the situation today. Everyone must find a way to save himself because the government has shown that it does not care about its own people. Life is only pain for us," he said in a resigned tone.

The next day Kiril stopped by wearing what I called his "millionaire attire." His Nike sneakers cost 2,000 rubles, a leather jacket 1,500, dark sunglasses, jeans, and an Italian shirt for another 1,500. When I whistled at his appearance, he said this was nothing compared to the suit he had recently bought from an Italian tourist. "When will you wear it?" I asked. He didn't know, but he said proudly, "In any case I will now look like a respectable businessman."

The real reason for his visit was not to show off his expensive clothes. "My father liked you. He had been expecting some kind of carefree, silly foreigner, but instead ..." "Has he gotten over the shock yet?" I interrupted. "He was very impressed, like my mother, and they hope you will visit us again," he said. I thanked him for the compliment and promised to come soon.

During the summer of 1991 I often passed Kiril doing business in front of the Beriozka shop. We would talk if he was alone. Otherwise I did not like to interrupt him during business hours. When it became colder he and his colleagues huddled together next to the radiator in the store and waited until they spotted a foreigner. Kiril's excellent English and charm won him customers, but his business still had its ups and downs. On some days his earnings from exchanging money and selling popular tourist items were over 1,000 rubles, and on other days nothing. His savings, which he kept at an undisclosed location, were adding up, and he hoped to buy a car within a year. He would need 50,000 rubles. When I gasped at this sum, knowing that the official price was considerably less, he laughed at my naïveté and said, "Growing inflation and increased bribes have pushed up the price of everything. It is not possible to enter a shop today and buy an item such as a car, refrigerator, or television without paying at least three times the official price."

The authority of the KGB and the Ministry of the Interior made me worry about Kiril. I knew that he had been picked up by the police a few times in the past and asked him when the last roundup had taken place. He admitted that a police jeep with the same two policemen came by weekly, and on the way to the precinct he and the other boys bought their freedom for 100 rubles. "What happens if other policemen pick you up who cannot be bribed?" I asked. He did not want to think about this, but his chewed fingernails indicated that he was not as calm as he appeared on the surface.

Another problem would arise when he reached his eighteenth birthday in November 1991. He would be conscripted into the army, unless he could prove he had a health problem. He was familiar with the methods other boys had used to be exempted from the army. Some feigned kidney problems by eating a kilo of sugar before the medical examination. Others pretended that they had tried to commit suicide by scarring their wrists with match burns. Some acted as though they were crazy and spent several months in a mental institution to escape service. Kiril had not chosen his method, but being a fatalist he believed everything would work out.

After almost one year on the job, Kiril could afford to live the life he had dreamed of as a child. "I can dress for 2,500 rubles, which is the price of the tape recorder my parents bought with their life savings," he said. "And I can sell my worn clothing at a profit at any time."

In order to convince me that his profession was prestigious, he cited an opinion poll published in *Komsomolskaya pravda,* in which youth chose black marketeering and prostitution as the two preferred professions among young people today. When I showed surprise about prostitution, Kiril said, "It is natural that a girl wants to be well dressed, and this requires foreign currency."

Kiril then painted a scene that sounded as though it came right out of Hollywood. "Just imagine, Lois, a poor girl walking down the street. She passes a prostitute who is wearing an Italian raincoat and elegant boots. Her Italian escort takes her arm, helps her into a foreign car, and they drive off. The girl, who comes from a working-class family, is envious of the prostitute, who comes from a similar background. She starts looking for foreigners who can give her this paradise in exchange for her services."

"Men have different needs," Kiril continued. "Those with little money are jealous of the black marketeer because he smokes foreign cigarettes and eats in the best restaurants. For Westerners this is nothing unusual. For Soviet youth it is a dream come true."

Kiril's earnings also permitted him to take a summer holiday in the Crimea with his girlfriend. She was a former classmate, who was studying to be a hairdresser. They had been together one year, and I asked him, rather boldly, if they were using any birth control measures. "I take care of this problem," he said, unembarrassed, "by bribing an employee in a drugstore." His girlfriend was much luckier than the majority of Soviet women, who must resort to abortion because birth control pills or devices are not available.

During his free time Kiril had a full schedule. Three times a week he attended a course for working teenagers at night school. In order to gain admittance, he had bought documents that certified he had an official job. The eighteen-month course would end soon, and he would receive a high school degree that would entitle him to a higher education. "This will always come in handy in case I decide to study one day," he said.

After night school he met other black marketeers whose gathering place was McDonald's. Kiril's more than seventy business colleagues had chosen this location, he said, "Because it is a piece of America. Everyone here likes American food and clothing."

Around the corner from my flat was another piece of America called Pizza Hut. One day Kiril invited me to be his guest there. Until then the long lines had discouraged me from entering the restaurant, but not

Kiril. This was where he and his friends ate regularly. The manager knew them and pocketed 10 rubles from each daily, so they did not have to line up.

The food was mediocre, but this was unimportant. The customers came for the typically American atmosphere with flashy colors and bright lighting, modern furnishings, and a scrubbed appearance. The staff had even learned to be polite, fast, and efficient, and the diners were able to relax for a few hours from the hardships of the gray world outside.

During lunch Kiril presented me with a beautiful Palekh brooch for my coming birthday. In spite of his attempt to be cheerful, I noticed that something was bothering him. After a while he revealed the reason. His friend Dima had been picked up by the police, who found $89 in his pocket. The court proceeding had just taken place, and he had been given a three-year prison sentence. Kiril was present at the trial, and he blamed Dima's mother for the severity of the punishment. She had told the judge that it was almost impossible to live honestly in this country and that hardly anyone was honest. "She spoke the truth," I said. "That is the reason he was punished." "Now you can understand why I want to leave," Kiril said.

2

THE ADVENTURER

*G*OOD MORNING, ADVENTURER. Are you packed and ready to go?" Masha asked in a chipper voice. I had been waiting the whole night for this call to confirm our weekend plans and was concerned that something had happened to Masha, whose life was an unending drama. "Sorry I could not phone earlier. I was hunting for a gas station that still had gas and got home at 2:30 with an empty tank." This reminded me of another ride with Masha—her car ran out of gas shortly before midnight, and we had to push it 100 meters to a gas station. Just before it was our turn the attendant closed the gas station, but not for long. Masha's pleas and tears earned her a full tank.

"Can you give me more information about our exact destination and departure time today?" I asked. A friend with connections had bought our train tickets and Masha did not have the details. She would be in touch in the afternoon.

Traveling with Masha, even in Moscow, is always an adventure. In the past, she had been stopped by the militia, had a flat tire, was sideswiped by a bus, lost her brakes, and a door refused to close. Recently she invited me to join her for a weekend excursion to the country. I accepted on the condition that she would not use her car. "The roads are too bad. We'll take a train," she said, to my relief. Masha had heard that dachas were selling for 600 rubles in a village whose name she had forgotten. She could not resist such a tempting bargain, even if it meant traveling nine hours by train to look at a cottage that was 400 kilometers northeast of Moscow.

Masha could visit all parts of her country, except for restricted military areas, but I had to follow the regulations for foreign correspondents. If I wanted to travel more than 40 kilometers from Moscow, I had to send a letter, not less than forty-eight hours before departure, to the person assigned to me in the Foreign Ministry and inform him of my exact travel plans. If I heard nothing from him, the trip was approved. To be on the safe side, I had already done this, but the letter did not contain details.

Shortly after Masha hung up, the responsible person from the Foreign Ministry called to ask about my exact train, destination, and hotel. I could not answer a single question and promised to call back as soon as I reached the Russian friend who had organized the trip. "I need this information before the end of the workday," he admonished, otherwise I would probably have to cancel the trip.

Shortly before 5:00 P.M. he called again, and I said in a resigned voice, "I've called everywhere, and no one knows where my friend is. I suppose I can't go." "This time we will make an exception," he said to my great surprise, "but the next time. ..." I was elated and said, "When I return I will give you all the information you need."

When Masha finally called that evening she sounded exhausted. After giving me the essential travel information, she found the energy for a rundown of the day's events.

It had been the last school day before her son's summer vacation, and a class party had been planned to honor those who had birthdays during the holidays. Masha was to buy fruit for the party, at a time when fruit was a rarity in stores.

After dropping her son off at school that morning, she had gone to the first large fruit and vegetable shop that she saw and had asked to speak with the director, whom she had never before seen. Her charming helplessness and big blue eyes won his sympathy and several kilos of oranges for the children. Then she asked, "Can I buy tomatoes for my family?" He agreed. In her high childlike voice, she thanked him and asked his name. "Can I come again, Victor?" He nodded and told her she was always welcome.

Knowing the rules of survival in the Soviet Union, I asked, "What did you give him?" "Absolutely nothing," she said emphatically. Masha was one of the few Russians I knew who accomplished most things by talking in such a persuasive way that it was almost impossible to say no.

It was already noon when she finally arrived at her office, and I asked how her boss reacted to her tardiness. "He has become accustomed to my irregular hours and doesn't object as long as I do my work." Then she added proudly, "Today I made all my important business calls from school." This was typical for Masha, who also used my apartment as an office. Whenever she came by during the workday, she made a beeline for the telephone to settle her business. Between calls and return calls we chatted and drank tea.

Masha was a journalist for a Moscow business magazine, and her busy schedule did not give her time to stand in lines, which she considered "just another profession." When her refrigerator was empty, she bought an extra portion of cheese or meat to take home to her son from the office canteen. Masha did not permit me to "waste" foreign currency on her in Beriozka shops, but she accepted products that I bought in neighborhood stores. In turn she often surprised me with my favorite spicy black bread or a jar of homemade jam made by a friend or relative.

Masha's work as a journalist gave her the opportunity to travel abroad, and after Masha returned from a month in America, her boss noticed a change in her. "Your eyes look free," he said. I understood what he meant. My Russian friends had made the same comment many years ago to point out the difference between us. When a taxi driver once asked me what country I came from, I countered with, "How do you know I am a foreigner?" "Look at the people on the streets. Can you see anyone with an open friendly face like yours? People are angry or tired, and their eyes are unsmiling." "I now look straight ahead and stand up with my shoulders back, like you," Masha said.

Other aspects of the American way of life also impressed her. "The Americans are so well-organized and have such a well-organized life. No one needs to sacrifice time, energy, or nerves to stand in lines. People are polite and disciplined and don't shout at each other. Americans know their rights and protest if they are violated; Russians are professional sufferers, who passively accept injustices as though they are normal," she said. The freedom of choice and feeling of responsibility in America were the most significant differences she noted. "In the Soviet Union we are accustomed to waiting for orders from above," she said.

The train was scheduled to leave at 1:45 and Masha promised to pick me up on time, which was an abstract idea for her. I was not unduly surprised, but nevertheless nervous when her delay caused us many near-accidents on the way to the railroad station. We were lucky; the train left ten minutes late, otherwise we would not have reached our sleeping car at the end of the train. We had hardly taken off our heavy rucksacks when the doors closed.

Masha knew the two boys who were already in the compartment. Twenty-two-year-old Kostya worked at a boarding school for orphaned, abandoned, and neglected children, where Alyosha, the other boy, a twelve-year-old, lived. They were going to spend the summer with Kostya's grandmother, with whom we planned to spend a few nights.

We were scheduled to arrive in Rossolovo at 11 the next morning, and Masha wanted to catch up on lost sleep. But there was a shouting match in the next compartment. Two people had been assigned the same berth, and neither was prepared to give it up. The train attendant finally convinced one that he would be given another place.

After solving this problem, the attendant brought us fresh sheets for 2 rubles a berth. The boys climbed to the upper berths, and we fell into the lower ones, exhausted. As the rhythm of the train lulled me to sleep, Masha whispered, "I'm too tired to sleep," and began chatting away. "Thanks to perestroika I can travel with you without fearing repercussions." This reminded me of an unforgettable trip I had made to Leningrad in the late 1970s with my Russian language teacher. When we returned to Moscow, she was publicly criticized at a party meeting and almost lost her job. Traveling with a foreigner without official permission was strictly forbidden back then.

One of Masha's hushed remarks surprised me. "Yesterday," she said, "I spent two hours at the militia station filling out forms in order to receive new documents." She had forgotten to tell me that someone had broken into her car not long before and had stolen all of her documents. For a moment I worried about what could happen if the police asked to see Masha's identification papers. Then I recalled how often she had been confronted with seemingly insurmountable obstacles and had miraculously overcome each one. Her greatest triumph, she admitted, was arranging sleeping quarters for a delegation of forty influential American

Jews, who arrived in summer when Moscow hotels were already booked. What did the ingenious Masha do? She hired an empty cruise ship, that just happened to be in port, as their hotel.

I awakened the following morning to French chansons emanating from the train's loudspeaker. The music complemented the simple pastoral scenes outside—carpets of daisies and buttercups, grazing cows, and farmers working their private plots. An old peasant woman sat on a bench bundled in a dark warm coat, scarf and galoshes next to her mummy-like husband, watching the world go by.

The idyllic scenes stopped momentarily when the train halted in the middle of nowhere to let passengers disembark. The passengers would cross the tracks and disappear into villages beyond view. At one station a horde of women were waiting for the train. As it screeched to a stop, they ran toward it with hands outstretched and waving. During that three-minute stop I watched them shove and elbow below an open window to buy a piece of meat from the train attendant. At other stations village dogs barked and waited for handouts.

When we finally arrived at the Rossolovo station, desolation and ugliness greeted us. The first signs of life were chickens and turkeys scratching for tidbits near the dirt platform. Rain from the night before had collected in deep puddles in front of a barnlike structure displaying the sign Rossolovo. The railroad station was empty, and the ticket window was closed. Only the train schedule posted on the wall connected this small town in Russia's heartland to such large cities as Leningrad, Moscow, and Sverdlovsk.

To our pleasant surprise, a pre-war vintage car was waiting to pick us up. Masha had called ahead to make this arrangement, but just in case it did not work out, she had prepared me for a possible 15-kilometer hike to our village. The boys preferred to walk, rather than to wait for us. The driver warned us that the rain had turned the roads to mud and made them impassable. He could take us only part of the way.

The ruts were so deep that I was afraid we would break an axle or find ourselves wallowing in mud. The car bounced and skidded uncomfortably, and I was grateful for distractions. We passed well-kept, wooden houses freshly painted dull red or gold. Their carved shutters, bordered in blue or green, were particularly charming. Picket fences separated one property from the next, and each household had its own small garden and mountain of wood for cooking and heating. Each house had a smaller, separate house with smoke coming out of its chimney. Masha explained that these were saunas.

When I saw people fetching water from a pump, I thought of the conveniences of urban life. It was a warm June day, and the driver told us the temperature could reach minus 30 degrees centigrade in winter. These poor people, I thought. They must freeze in their outhouses. The road was empty except for the occasional motorcycle. Some had sidecars for their goggled passengers; they reminded me of German army patrols in World War II films.

From time to time the road filled with barking dogs that chased us. Being a dog lover, I had noticed during my travels throughout Russia that each village seemed to have its own original mixture of dog; I saw prestigious purebreds only in cities.

On the outskirts of Rossolovo we crossed over a river and into the countryside on a newly constructed steel bridge that brought me back to the twentieth century. The steel bridge replaced the nearby dilapidated wooden bridge from which a wizened man fished. We soon reached a point where the road disappeared under water, forcing the driver to stop. He pointed us in the direction that we should walk, and I saw only flat green fields ahead and no signs of life. After giving Masha the key to the 600-ruble dacha, he wished us luck.

I suddenly remembered Masha's telephone call just the day before, that had begun, "Good morning, adventurer." At that moment I had thought she was joking, but now I realized she might have been serious, and I had an uneasy feeling. We had just begun to hike, when a mirage appeared. I rejoiced when I saw that it was a truck coming our way. Masha flagged it down, and the driver could not refuse her entreaty to make a short detour through soaked fields to the village. He seemed ill at ease, and, while he and Masha talked, he concealed the right side of his face with his hand. During the drive, however, he had to put both hands on the steering wheel, and he could no longer hide the ugly black and blue bruise that covered his cheek. His left hand was wrapped in a now-dry, but blood-soaked bandage. Masha immediately asked him about his injuries, and he told her that the day before he had driven 170 kilometers to buy vodka. The line was long when he got there, so he asked if he could go to the front because he had come from so far away. This enraged a few of the men who had been waiting for hours, and they beat him up.

After bumping and zigzagging through the fields, we reached a cluster of dilapidated houses, their roofs collapsing. Several with closed shutters looked abandoned. One of the two that looked habitable was Masha's "bargain." It was a log cabin; the roof was a little lopsided, but this was minor compared to the condition of its rooms. Dampness had caused the beams to rot and the wallpaper to sag in many places. The only signs of life were spider webs and three odd shoes, which apparently belonged to former residents. The dacha would require major repairs, and since it was almost impossible to procure building materials, Masha decided not to buy it. "I hope you are not disappointed," she said to me. I understood that she was trying to conceal her own disappointment and said, "I am looking forward to meeting Kostya's grandmother."

No roads led to the grandmother's village, but before leaving, the truck driver pointed us in the right direction. Once again I saw a green ocean— flat fields undulating in the breeze. After walking at least 3 kilometers, with rucksacks laden with provisions for our hostess, we finally saw the first signs of village life. Cows and goats grazed near a farmhouse, and the wind wafted the pungent odor of dung toward us.

In contrast to the empty fields, the village was bursting with activity. Freshly washed laundry waved in the breeze. Squawking chickens scurried for food scraps, children played hide-and-seek, and a robust woman passed us balancing pails of water at either end of a pole over her shoulder. Masha had visited this village the year before and recognized the green wooden house with a gray roof as that of Anna Ivanova, Kostya's grandmother.

She waited for us on her front porch. Next to her stood a gaping reception committee composed of our two companions from the train, her daughter, Natasha, and a handful of children. They had all come from Moscow to spend their summer holidays in the countryside.

Before entering the house we took off our muddy shoes and left them on the porch, replacing them with one of the many pairs of worn slippers lined up in front of the door. Our hostess, Anna Ivanova, noticed that we looked tired and insisted that we relax while she set the table. I counted nine heads and wondered where everyone was to sleep in a house that appeared to have only one large room furnished with a dining table, cupboard, and sofa. Natasha must have read my thoughts. The sofa would be my bed, she explained, and Masha's was tucked away in a corner near the room's entrance. She pulled aside a curtain that concealed a tiny room with beds side by side. The boys had the coziest place in the house—they were to sleep in a warm niche above the tiled stove.

Natasha's openness and warmth made me feel at home at once. She even made an effort to speak English, which she had learned in grammar school some thirty years before. Being a practical woman, she began with the essentials. She showed us the way to the toilet. Farmhouses used to be built with adjoining quarters for animals and people; the toilet was located where the animals lived. Natasha led us through a corridor and down steps into a part of the house that looked like a barn. It was now used to store chopped wood, broken furniture, conserves, and bikes. The toilet, which consisted of a seat on top of a square metal box, was in a dark corner.

Natasha planned to stay only for the weekend, but, "Two days here are like a week of vacation," she said. Her mother had arrived from Moscow in April and would remain until October; she belonged to the increasing number of pensioners who are bringing the ghost villages of the Russian countryside back to life. Some of the old people in this village, like Anna Ivanova, were from Moscow, and others from Leningrad, but most had grown up in the countryside. During the twilight of their lives, they wanted to return to nature, work the land, and escape the pollution and fast tempo of city life. Unlike their children and grandchildren, their needs were modest, and they were content to lead a simple rural life.

Anna Ivanova refused our help in the kitchen, and I respected her wishes reluctantly. I had learned that in Russia guests know their place. In my apartment my close friends always took over some kitchen duties, but a stranger never lifted a finger.

I noticed that most of the food on the table came from Moscow; bread, Natasha told me, was the only product bought locally, and it came from a village 3 kilometers away. Masha and I had brought tea and cans of meat and fish for our hostess. During the summer they would live from their garden, which Anna Ivanova had planted with onions, lettuce, tomatoes, cucumbers, strawberries, and cabbage. At the end of the season they would not be able to carry more than a sack of potatoes, onions, and garlic back to Moscow. The villagers dream of the day when a road will be built that will enable them to transport the fruits of their labor home. These provisions would help them to survive the hard winter, when fruits and vegetables are a luxury.

Everyone was talking at the same time at the table, and I had difficulty following the conversations. This gave me time to focus on the family ancestors who stared at me from frames on the wall. Among the portraits hung bunches of dried flowers and scenes of the countryside painted by Natasha. A candle burned below two religious scenes in the "icon corner," a tradition in farmhouses.

The arrival of a plain-looking farmhand dressed in a torn shirt and blue, holey jogging pants brought my attention back to the table. This was Sergei, a nephew of Anna Ivanova, who carried in a large jar of unpasteurized milk. While the children gulped down the milk, I sipped slowly, trying to remember when I had last tasted milk straight from a cow.

Sergei had left Moscow three months before to settle in a nearby village, where he worked on a kolkhoz, a collective farm, raising milk cows. "What made you move?" I asked. Before he answered my question he told me a little about himself. "I am not an educated man, but my former profession taught me a little about life," he said. Sergei had worked in Moscow as a waiter in hotel restaurants for foreigners for twenty years. "For my whole life I have been intimidated by one thing or another. At work the KGB warned me not to have private conversations with foreigners, who could be spies. It took me more than forty years to be free of fears," he said. Natasha interrupted to say, "Five years ago I would not have dared to speak freely to a foreigner or even sleep under the same roof."

Sergei left city life because of his love of nature and the feeling of freedom it gave him. He also wanted to break his drinking habit. His dream was to be a private farmer and own a herd of cows, but this was not as easy as he had imagined. "The people here are in a deep slumber. They are not interested in founding a cooperative and earning a good living as free people. The only thing they want to do is drink."

I was familiar with the drinking problem that has paralyzed the work force in the Soviet Union for decades. Monotony and the hardships of life drive many to seek consolation in the bottle. When alcohol is not available the hard drinkers are known to consume everything from window-cleaning fluid to eau de cologne, methanol, auto coolants, and brake fluid.

"Many people want to have their own businesses and have the energy and know-how to help put this country back on its feet economically," Sergei said, "but our system does not permit this. For seventy-three years the party has brought us nothing except misery, and it continues to stand in the way of those who show initiative. When a person works for himself he works harder."

English journalist David Satter described the problems of Soviet agriculture in an article published in 1989. He wrote that the problems can be traced to the 1920s when a free agricultural market was considered a threat to the party. Stalin responded by exiling many farmers to Siberia and forcing others to become members of kolkhozes. Between 1932 and 1933, 7 million farmers died of starvation. Those who survived became rural slaves. Satter quoted Anatoly Strelyani, a Soviet agricultural expert, who said, "In essence the farmer works for a bureaucrat instead of for himself. This makes him indifferent to the land. It's unnatural to farm in a prison."

Through the system of central planning, orders come from Moscow, which can lead to absurd situations. For example, when the ministry in

Moscow decides that seeds should be planted in April, although the soil is still frozen in some parts of the country, regional officials pass on these instructions to kolkhoz chairmen. Neither would consider questioning orders from above for fear of jeopardizing their position, so they command farmers to start planting. The farmers recognize this foolishness, and either they work poorly or not at all.

It is officially estimated that after the harvest is in, at least 30 percent of the fresh fruit, vegetable, potato, and grain crops spoil, although I had heard unofficially in 1991 that 50 percent is a more realistic figure. The reasons read like a list of illnesses. Only 20 percent of the roads are paved, so it is difficult to move the products. Then there are too few trucks, too few warehouses and cold-storage facilities, old and faulty equipment, a shortage of workers, and on and on.

After having a quick bite, Sergei rushed back to work. We remained at the table listening to the gregarious Natasha air her practical views. "The more money a person has, the more wishes he has. We have tolerated a hard life because we did not have a chance to make wishes. The whole country lived like a large poor family that has nothing and wants nothing. As soon as a person possesses more, the neighbor begins to hate him."

During my years in Moscow I have noticed that envy is the most venomous Soviet disease. There is even a cynical saying that describes this mentality. When someone's cow dies, the neighbor rejoices. A Russian friend, who had been to Western Europe, said, "In the West envy also exists, but it usually has a positive influence. If a family lives well, the neighbor will work hard to improve his life-style. In the Soviet Union the mentality is different. If a family has a beautiful new car the neighbor, who hasn't one, will try to damage it."

After lunch Kostya proposed that Masha and I take a walk with him along the river. On our way we met a little old lady, who was resting. She had just finished turning the hay in her field with a wooden pitchfork. The hay would be winter feed for her goat, which grazed nearby. She wore a white scarf and a printed apron that protected what was likely her one and only dress. Her skin was weathered and I had difficulty guessing her age. She greeted us in a faltering, ancient voice, and I took the opportunity to talk with her. The village had been her home for more than eighty years. She had never married, and the only family she had were nephews and nieces, who visited her occasionally. Neighbors also came by from time to time and brought her water and bread. "Today I had no bread so I made blini. Life here is hard in winter and the village is practically empty. But you see, my dear, I am still on my feet."

Her workday had begun at 5:00 A.M., and she complained that she had slept badly because her legs ached. I glanced at her crippled, bowed legs and wondered how she could walk at all. She said she would quit early today and invited us to visit her house. We couldn't refuse and followed her. A crooked wooden stick supported her as she tottered along behind the goat, which led the way home. "The house with the yellow mailbox nailed to the door is mine," she said. Why did she need a mailbox? I thought. Newspapers were not delivered to small villages, and I assumed that mail service had been discontinued a long time ago. She reached into the box and took out the key.

Her house had two rooms, which were amazingly orderly and spick-and-span. A candle burned in front of two icons on the wall in the icon corner. "That is where I pray daily," she said and crossed herself. She proudly showed me her refrigerator, black-and-white television, and radio, whose blaring made it difficult for me to hear her. "You see, I have everything," she said.

"Once a month I go to the store with my ration coupons. Without them I could buy nothing. They entitle me to sugar and soap. There is not much more in the store. I can also buy vodka with the coupons. I don't drink, but I always save a bottle for the worker who brings me wood for my stove, and another for the man who helps me plant potatoes in my garden. No law states that I must do this, but if I did not do it, no one would help me."

I was touched by the modest needs of this old woman. Many other villagers whom I had met during my travels in the Soviet Union complained bitterly about their life. Some even longed for the days of Stalin. I remembered a pensioner who said, "Stalin did a great deal for us. After the war there was a time when we did not have ration cards, and the shops were much fuller than today. Now the press explains to the youth that Stalin was bad. We old people remember mainly his good side."

The old woman showed me her kitchen and I was pleased to see that it was as cluttered as mine. An old samovar stood next to a plate of cold blini that she had fried that morning. Her daily food staples were stored in pails and jars on the counters and floor. I could see at a glance that her diet consisted of potatoes, cabbage, honey, and milk from her goat. Eventually the goat would provide her with meat, she said. She had heard about city people who came to villages to buy eggs, milk, and chickens. She had prepared cabbage for the coming winter and asked if we knew of anyone who might want to buy her sauerkraut. In a large earthenware pot were kilos of dried cubes of bread, which she hoped would also see her through the winter.

She recalled a time when the neighboring village had sixty horses, and every family had at least two cows. "That was before the revolution and the introduction of kolkhozes, which destroyed our agriculture and drove the farmers from the land," she said. "But I have remained and don't want to leave. I can still work in the fields, gather firewood, and feed my goat, which gives me milk. This is the place where I will die."

It was getting late and we had to leave. I was sad, because I knew that she belonged to a generation that was dying out.

Kostya led us along the narrow path that paralleled the meandering river. After several minutes we found a comfortable place to sit in the sun and talk. His father was a teacher who also repaired technical equipment at the same boarding school where Kostya worked. Kostya often organized activities for the 150 children, between the ages of four and fourteen, who lived there. All came from troubled backgrounds, and the parents of some children were alcoholics, criminals, or ill and were deemed unfit to raise their children.

As I listened, I thought how fortunate those children were to have Kostya as an example for the future. He was honest, hardworking, and had a strong sense of right and wrong. He criticized young people his age who were only interested in clothing and other material goods. One of his friends, a black marketeer, had earned 20,000 rubles with which he bought a ticket to Brussels. Now he was in Brussels without a kopeck in his pocket. "He never learned how to work. The West doesn't need such a person. Just imagine, if our shops were suddenly full of goods, the black marketeers would be unemployed."

By the time we returned home the air was chilly and I was shivering. Masha proposed that we warm up in the sauna located in a small wooden house across the street. I had often visited saunas in Moscow that consisted of rooms for showering, perspiring, and resting, but I had never been in a village sauna. I had to bend down to enter a small dark room where we undressed and left our clothing on a wooden bench. The adjoining room was the sauna. The pleasant smell of birch emanating from the hot coals was inebriating. The floor was covered with hay to absorb the alternating pails of cold and warm water that we poured over ourselves. From time to time we beat our skin with a bunch of leafy birch branches. "That is good for blood circulation," Masha said.

The sauna was so relaxing that I wanted to go to bed at once, but I was not allowed to skip dinner. Once again the table was filled with food.

I looked forward to a deep sleep after an ample dose of country air, a generous meal, and the relaxing sauna, but the mosquitoes had other plans. Of the nine people in the house, I was the one they selected to terrorize. I sought shelter under the covers, but whenever I surfaced for air, mosquito troops were waiting to attack. The next morning my body looked like a cranberry bush in autumn.

Masha told me about one family she had visited the year before. She referred to them as the "elite of the village," and we decided to visit them. They lived in a solidly built, well-preserved, seventy-year-old house. "Now you can see how houses used to be built," she said. As soon as a new apartment building is completed in Moscow, repairs are necessary. This house, like others in the village, was a log cabin.

At our knock Nina, the housewife, greeted Masha warmly and welcomed us into her spacious living room, which was filled with antique furniture and the framed faces of ancestors. I was a little too enthusiastic about the furniture and earned a detailed explanation about every piece.

The crystal chandelier, desks, chairs, and commode were from St. Petersburg, she said, using the original name for the city that became Leningrad in 1924 and once again bears that name. The sewing machine bore the label Original Victorian. The grandfather clock's loud gong every half hour reminded us that it was still alive. "Russians used to be wonderful craftsmen, but now they don't know what it means to work," Nina said.

She had lived in the house until 1956, when her family received an apartment in Moscow. "Thanks to the generosity of the Soviet government, we were given a flat in the city, and now we can spend summers in the village." Ira, her daughter-in-law, laughed sarcastically at this remark and said, "You are grateful because you have never experienced a better life. As long as you are not threatened by starvation, war, or imprisonment, you are content. At your age you should rest and not work so hard." "That's a fine idea," her mother-in-law answered. "That would mean that children would do the heavy work and give us a chance to rest, but they don't do that." Ira wisely changed the subject, but Nina continued in a loud, excited voice. "I have worked my entire life and that is probably the reason why I don't have problems. I never considered clothes important or wore fashionable jeans, and I don't feel I have missed anything."

Life had become more difficult in the village, she admitted, because of the shortage of goods, and, unlike her eighty-two-year-old neighbor, she lived mainly on supplies that she and relatives brought from Moscow. Fresh vegetables from the garden were the exception. She recalled nostalgically the days when thirty families lived in the village and when it had its own store that sold butter and cheese. Now there were only ten people who lived here year-round, she said, and most of them were women over seventy who received a monthly pension of 70 rubles and relied on their children to help them out. "Many young people left the village to receive a higher education," Nina said, "and they never returned." "Who wants to work a twelve-hour day for only a few kopecks? If the government paved roads to villages, built adequate living quarters and entertainment facilities, and permitted private ownership of land, the young people would return to the countryside," Ira said.

Our weekend was coming to an end, and we had a long trek to the nearest bus station. I was sorry to leave such wonderful people, whom I most likely would never see again. While a tear ran down Anna Ivanova's cheek, she said, "God be with you," and crossed herself. Natasha, Kostya, and Alyosha insisted on accompanying us to the bus stop. On the way we passed acres of potato fields belonging to the kolkhoz and walked through carpets of wildflowers, some of which Masha picked for a bouquet. I anticipated at least a 5-kilometer hike, when once again a moving object appeared on the horizon. I could see only fields in that direction, but then noticed a narrow, dirt road on which a car made slow progress toward us. As the car came closer I saw that it already had two sturdy men and a solidly built woman inside. The seemingly full car did not stop Masha from waving it down. The passengers agreed to take us to town, and I rejoiced once again at our luck.

I had difficulty understanding the rural dialect of our new companions and was constantly distracted by a strange noise that sounded like a grunting pig. I began to doubt my sanity, when the woman in the front seat screamed. From under her seat emerged a squeaking piglet that had just bitten her leg. Next to dogs, pigs are my favorite animals, and Masha feared that we would return to Moscow with a new pet. If they had told us that the little creature was going to be grilled that day, her concern would have been justified. We were relieved to learn that they had just bought the piglet for 25 rubles and planned to keep it for breeding.

Once again the ticket office at the railroad station was closed. The cashier had gone shopping and would return soon, a villager mumbled. We had time to spare and decided to take a walk in the gray, depressing town. The most activity was at the food shop, which we entered by balancing on a narrow board across a two-day-old puddle. On the wall was a large sign listing the amount of rationed products each customer could buy. The few non-rationed items on the shelves, such as dry soups, tomato and pea conserves, and Turkish tea, were caked with dust and looked as though they had been there for years.

When we returned to the railroad station the ticket office was open, and the cashier told us that our train would be an hour late. We figured we had a good two hours to kill, and Masha proposed that we visit a milk factory only a kilometer away, which she had visited the year before. We walked down a muddy road past green backyards planted with rows of potatoes and a variety of vegetables that would most likely see the towns-people through the long, hard winter.

During Masha's last visit she had met Yuri, the factory's director, and when we arrived, she asked to see him. He was not in, but his brother, Rassul, his assistant, was delighted to show a foreign journalist the fac-tory. While walking from one room to the next I thought that the factory would not have met even the most lax Western sanitary regulations. It did not even surprise me when Rassul put his unwashed hand into the re-volving tank where cheese was being made.

We still had time before our train departed, and Rassul invited us to his brother's home, where he also lived. We interrupted Yuri's shy wife, who was ironing in the living room while her three-year-old son sat mes-merized by karate on television. We sat down on the sofa, the only piece of furniture in the room, and chatted until Yuri arrived. The family was now complete, and I noticed that they did not appear to be ethnic Rus-sians—they were short, dark Mediterranean types, with slightly slanted eyes. They told me that they were Karabaschew and that their home was in the Caucasus.

The job as director of the milk factory had brought Yuri to Rossolovo six years before, but now he was fed up and ready to return home. "All the changes of the last six years have made life and work more difficult," he said in a quiet, resigned voice. "It was easier when the administration had the authority to make demands on the workers and force them to work according to certain standards. Now they can vote the boss out of office. At present I can accomplish nothing because the workers have more rights than I do."

"I am a party member but believe the future role of the party is only ideological. It should no longer mix in economics—that sphere belongs to economic experts. Previously the party placed its own people in lead-ing positions and many were unqualified. The workers must have full stomachs before they will be willing to work well. Over the past months, my employees have become angrier and more aggressive because they cannot clothe and feed their families." Russian customers regularly insulted his wife while she was shopping and complained that they had "less to eat because you black people are coming and eating our food."

Seventy-five percent of the production in Yuri's milk factory was sent to other republics, he said. "We are officially left with nothing. We should be producing 50 percent more, but we lack equipment and workers. The situation is so bad that the kolkhoz chairman asks bookkeepers to milk cows during the lunch break."

In order to satisfy his employees' needs Yuri made an unofficial agreement with a chicken farm. "We give them milk products and receive meat in return. The villages would like to have their own pig or cow, but the kolkhoz does not permit privately owned animals to graze on its land. At the same time milk and meat are not for sale in shops. We must replace the old system with a new one, but this has not been possible until now."

Yuri made one last call to the railroad station to inquire about our train's arrival time. He was told that it would arrive in an hour. Since we wanted to be ahead of time, we started walking toward the railroad station. The noise of a passing train distracted us for a second, and Masha joked, "That was probably our train."

When we arrived at the railroad station, we learned that it was not a joke. The cashier said that our train had been on time, and that she was not to blame for the inaccurate information. "I shouldn't have believed them. They never tell the truth," Masha shouted and burst into laughter a few minutes later. "We had a journalist's luck. We had a good interview and missed the train."

The next train was scheduled to arrive at 4:30 P.M., which meant waiting another four hours. It was lunchtime and not a soul was on the street. We stretched out on the peeling, listing benches in front of the railroad station, and the warm sun made us sleepy. Even the clucking pigeons could not keep us awake.

The noise of arriving passengers woke us. Masha entered the station and told those who were lining up in front of the closed ticket window that we were first in the queue, and no one objected. Queuing in the Soviet Union has its own rules, which I quickly learned. One can leave the line and return to the same place several minutes, or hours, later, as long as the person behind you agrees.

Masha saw no need for me to stand with her and assigned me to the hard bench to guard our belongings. I was not within hearing distance, but noticed that she was involved in an intense discussion with a middle-aged man. He had a blond moustache and was unshaven; he wore a black leather jacket, soiled trousers, and sneakers. She left the line suddenly and rushed over to me. Her pale face and uncharacteristically severe expression told me that something was amiss. "That ugly man," and she pointed in his direction, "is an anti-Semite. He asked me where I came from and when I said Moscow, he replied, 'Why have you come to this town instead of going to Israel?'" "Why do I have to go to Israel?" she asked. "That is your motherland, where you belong," he replied.

I have always been a defender of the underdog and said I would settle the matter. I went up to him and asked why he had insulted my friend. "I didn't mean to insult her when I said, 'You are a child of Israel.' I can see nationality on a person's face, although it is unusual for a Jew to have blue eyes."

This rough-looking type was also critical of Russians. "They have permitted everything to deteriorate in their republic. In my hometown, Tallinn [Estonia], the buildings are well kept, the streets clean, the people polite, and teenagers have cafés where they can spend their leisure time. In Russia there is no place where a person can relax and feel like a human being. The government has so much money. Why can't it do something for its people? We are living in a feudal state where everyone is a slave. The laws have no meaning and there is no authority here. Only a person with money has rights." Even though I disliked him, I had to admit that he spoke the truth, which I had heard many times.

The noise of the train's arrival interrupted our conversation, and Masha rushed ahead to save two seats. The train was full of weekenders returning from outings. They were still in a holiday mood and their portable radios were blasting. Freshly picked wildflowers were lying under seats next to cloth-covered pails. It was too early to pick mushrooms, so the contents of the pails remained a mystery.

Our train took us 30 kilometers closer to Moscow. Masha hoped that we could board a direct train to Moscow at the next station, but there was no such train. While considering the alternatives we ate pickles and boiled potatoes, which we bought from a villager on the platform. The long day had begun at 8 A.M., and it was unclear where and when we would have our next meal.

A parked intercity bus inspired Masha to decide that we would cover the next stretch by bus, and she begged the driver to take us aboard. At first he was reluctant because there was only standing room and the aisle was already full. It did not take long, however, before he became the umpteenth person to give in to Masha's persuasive charm. We squeezed in and the next two hours were an endurance test. We bounced from side to side, practically falling into the laps of those in seats, and we could rest only when the bus broke down.

Each man on board then advised the driver what he should do, and eventually, through some miracle, the engine started, and we continued the journey through the green, uninhabited countryside. We reached the next stop too late to make a train connection to Moscow, and Masha once again found a way out of a dilemma. We would go by car to Yaroslavl, the next large city with regular train service to Moscow.

After bargaining with taxi drivers about the cost of the ride, she chose a private driver who asked for 20 rubles, half the amount that his competition had demanded. Had I known that he would spend the next two hours cursing the government and Gorbachev and not give me a moment's sleep, I would have paid more, just to have had peace.

We arrived in Yaroslavl at 11:30 P.M. and joined the long line in front of the ticket window. A train to Moscow was scheduled to leave soon, and we hoped that there would be places for us. Just before our turn, seven friends joined the man standing in front of me, and they bought the last available seats. Their appearance told everyone in line that they were from the Caucasus, and suddenly I heard racist remarks directed at them, which they simply ignored.

Masha had still not given up and ran to a window where people return tickets. We were lucky. She bought the last two, and we raced to the train. The first-class sleeping compartments, which we had enjoyed on the way to Rossolovo, were booked up, so we sat in second class on stiff, hard seats for the next several hours.

At 5 A.M. we finally arrived in Moscow dirty, exhausted, and aching, and my only thought was bed. But first we had to find a way to get home. The buses and Metro begin running at 6 A.M., and at least one hundred people were standing in front of the taxi stand. The only alternative was to find a private driver. We refused the first, who asked us for a sum equivalent to a third of an average monthly salary. Finally a young man took pity on us and asked for a modest amount. As we parted at 6 A.M. Masha said, "There's a dacha I want to look at next weekend. Do you want to join me again?"

3

MISS PERESTROIKA

*L*ARISSA'S LIFE reads like a success story. Her recipe has been hard work and perseverance. But above all, perestroika gave her the opportunity to become an esteemed sociologist and journalist.

She was born in 1945 in a small Russian town, a 24-hour train ride from Moscow. Her family was poor and her mother had no time to care for her. A few weeks after her birth Larissa was left with her grandmother who raised her up until her late teens.

"The happiest period in my life was my childhood," Larissa said. She and her grandmother lived together in a clay house with a chalk-white facade and red tiled roof. They had two small rooms but usually used only one. "This saved my grandmother the chore of feeding two coal stoves," she said. In the backyard was the outhouse they built together, but the grandmother, who was only 150 centimeters [4 feet 9 inches] tall, did not have the strength to dig a well. Larissa's main household chore was to fetch water from a nearby pump. They could not irrigate a garden without a well, so their yard looked like a forest, which upset the neighbors. Unlike other children, Larissa was allowed to run barefoot in her "jungle," as she called it, and this was her first taste of freedom.

Her grandmother had only a few months of schooling, but in that short time she developed a love of reading, which she passed on to her granddaughter. They had their own small library at home and Larissa spent most of her time reading. This gave the neighbors another reason to criticize her grandmother. "How can you permit Larissa to read so much? She will damage her eyes," they said. The grandmother wore thick glasses and this was proof to them that reading was harmful. They also reproached the indulgent grandmother for treating Larissa like a "princess." It would be better, they said, if she had a practical upbringing like their children; she should clean up the backyard and do housework.

Larissa was not cut out for village life, and her admittance to Moscow University, the most prestigious in the country, gave her the chance, at eighteen, to fulfill her first dream. She wanted to live in a big city. She graduated with a history degree and qualified to teach German history in the German language, but teaching did not interest her. She decided to continue her studies in sociology and philosophy, and earned a Ph.D.

While a student she met her future husband, a Russian classmate, and married at the age of twenty-seven. "He was the love of my life," she said, "but something went wrong, and after seven years of marriage I asked for a divorce." At first he was opposed to the divorce, and when she did not change her mind, he sought revenge. The legal proceedings took five years and were covered in Moscow newspapers. The issue involved a Muscovite marrying a non-Muscovite. Many Soviet citizens born in cities other than Moscow want to live and work in the capital, but this requires a residence permit, which is exceedingly difficult to procure. "Business marriages" are illegal, but many use them in order to obtain the right to live in Moscow.

Larissa's husband maintained that she was "a cunning Jew" who had married him in order to receive official permission to live in Moscow. He hoped the judge would expel her from Moscow on the basis of this argument. Her friends then came to her defense, and he lost the case.

After the divorce Larissa experienced the fate of many divorced women. She was forced to continue living with her former husband because of the shortage of living space in Moscow. After two years she was able to make a complicated apartment exchange, which gave her a room of her own in a communal flat. Larissa shared the kitchen, bathroom, and corridor with a married couple who also had a room of their own in the apartment.

New problems arose after this move. Her new neighbor, Tamara, was an anti-Semite, but this was not the first time that Larissa had experienced anti-Semitism. When she was a child other children had thrown stones at her, calling her a Jew. Legally she was a Russian, like her mother and grandmother, and this was written in her passport. But she bore the name of her Jewish father. "Here they judge by the nose, not by the nationality written in the passport," she said.

Tamara welcomed Larissa with the comment, "We had no cockroaches in my apartment before you arrived. Where Jews live there are cockroaches," and she pointed to one that was running through the kitchen. Larissa was deeply hurt at the time, but today she jokes and says, "I was not aware that so many Jews live in Moscow."

Tamara's explanation reminded me of an experience I had while living in China during the early 1970s. When I complained about the cockroaches that covered the kitchen wall like wallpaper, the Chinese said that foreigners had brought them into the country in their baggage.

Larissa and her neighbor had different working and living styles. Tamara worked as a cleaning woman in a military hospital that was located an hour and a half by subway from the apartment. She left home at 7 A.M. and returned at 7 P.M.; her bedtime was no later than 10 P.M.

Larissa was a sociologist at the Academy of Sciences and spent long days and nights working at home or in the library. This was preferable to sharing a 16-square-meter [52-square-foot] office at her institute with twenty-six colleagues. Her boss expected her to appear twice a week to discuss her work.

Tamara was suspicious of Larissa since she did not go to an office on weekdays. She also disapproved of her entertaining guests in the evening. She especially disapproved of guests who had beards, which she associated with dissidents, or who were fashionably dressed like black marketeers.

Tamara, ostensibly as a good citizen, wrote to the police precinct in her district and asked the officers to investigate Larissa's work habits. The policeman who appeared at the door one day already knew Tamara. He was assigned to the building and in the past had been called in when Tamara's former husband became rowdy or beat her up.

He informed Larissa about Tamara's letter and reminded her of his responsibility to enforce the law that every healthy person of working age must be employed. In response to his question about her source of income, Larissa showed the policeman her working papers. He blushed when he saw that she was employed at one of the most prestigious institutes in the country, and he apologized. Then he turned on Tamara, raging, "You old_____ If you insult your decent neighbor once again I will fine you 50 rubles."

Tamara's failure to enlist the policeman's support did not stop her from continuing to insult Larissa. "You behave as though you are important and intelligent. You can't fool me," she said one day. The problem between workers and intellectuals was not new to me. I had often heard intellectuals remark, "We don't speak the same language," although both workers and intellectuals spoke Russian. Larissa explained that since the 1917 revolution, workers had been told that intellectuals could not be trusted because they could deceive and exploit the workers with their cleverness. Their different life-styles and interests made intellectuals appear to be arrogant, and this was another reason to distrust them.

Sometimes Tamara's new husband, who was considerably more educated than Tamara, would come into the kitchen during one of her frequent diatribes against Larissa and demand that she be quiet. Occasionally he would lock her up in their room if she did not stop, and then he would apologize to Larissa.

The blond and hefty Tamara seldom showed any consideration for her neighbor and sometimes behaved as though all of the communal space in the apartment was hers. She would use the bathtub for several hours to soak her wash, hang her dripping clothes in the kitchen, use all four burners of the stove to boil clothes and to cook for the week, fill the corridor with her belongings, and even throw Larissa's belongings on the floor.

After five years relations between the women took a gradual turn for the better. Larissa attributed the change to the influence of Tamara's husband. One evening, when Tamara was not aware that Larissa was home, Larissa overheard a telephone conversation through the thin wall of their adjoining rooms. "My neighbor is well informed and said ... Incidentally, did you see her on television yesterday?"

A hand-delivered invitation by a driver from the German embassy to Larissa and the coming and going of foreigners convinced Tamara that her neighbor was a VIP. She began to treat her with a new respect and even volunteered occasionally to wash the floor when it was Larissa's turn. Over time Tamara showed her growing trust by discussing private matters with her. She talked about family problems and about the apartment that she and her husband hoped to receive. She even asked Larissa for help. Using Larissa's first name and patronymic to show her respect, she said, "Larissa Lvovna, you can write very well. Can you please write a letter for me?"

On another occasion Tamara's husband, a retired army officer, talked with Larissa about Soviet history. "Larissa Lvovna, I want you to tell me honestly without talking around the subject, did we free Germany and other socialist countries?" Larissa answered, "The Soviet Union defeated fascism, but we did not free other countries. To the contrary, we installed our own kind of fascism through the repressive methods of Stalin. We do not have an accurate picture of what the Americans and the other allies did. This has been concealed from the people."

The former officer listened attentively and said, "That is a completely different matter. You have not answered my question. Did we free Germany from fascism or not?" The conversation ended unsatisfactorily, and Larissa's comment later was, "The historical revelations since glasnost shattered his view of the world and everything he formerly believed in and fought for. He does not understand why those who were formerly repressed as enemies have now been rehabilitated and are martyrs. His heroes, Stalin and Lenin, have been denounced and stand on the gallows. Unlike Tamara, who thinks only about her immediate living and shopping problems, he is experiencing a personal trauma."

I also noticed a change in Tamara's behavior. Previously she would greet me grudgingly or simply hang up the telephone when she heard my voice. Now when I called and Larissa was not home, she would act like a private secretary who did not know when to stop talking. At the end of a conversation she would say, "Larissa and I are looking forward to seeing you."

The one person Larissa did not want to see was her mother, who, she said, brought out her worst traits. Larissa was usually tolerant of people, but when the subject "mother" entered the conversation she became almost hysterical. Her face, normally serene, would become tortured, and her soft, melodic voice became high-pitched. Even the dimple in the middle of her chin would deepen. She remembered that her happy childhood with her grandmother was interrupted once a year by her mother. At first she could hardly wait to see her, but, when she finally arrived, harmony vanished, and Larissa would want her to leave. Both her grandmother and her mother were stubborn and uncompromising, and they fought during the entire visit.

Larissa knew her mother only through these annual visits and the bulky letters she sent, instructing her how to behave. Now Larissa criticized her mother for ending her studies so early. "If my mother had gone to school for more than five years, she would have had a proper profession instead of being only a singer in a cultural brigade," Larissa said. Her mother's work in a traveling theater company kept her on the road, and she used this as the excuse to deposit her three daughters, one after another, with her mother. "The truth is," Larissa said quietly, while staring at the floor, "she never loved me and that is why she abandoned me."

When they were together, they argued about everything, from her mother's short skirts to her belief in Stalin, who was a hero for her generation. Even though she now condemned him, she did not understand why Larissa criticized her for singing Stalinist songs to her grandchildren.

"Mother never tries to change or improve herself," Larissa said in a resigned tone. "Why can't you accept her the way she is?" I asked. "I can accept other people, but she is a part of my past from which I have struggled to escape. I hate myself for my intolerance and dogmatism, which are characteristics I inherited from her. I have spent many years fighting against the person I was. I have found friends who are examples for me. You and others have taught me how to behave and how to dress properly. Many doors would be closed to me today if I still looked like a villager."

Over the past few years Larissa has gained self-confidence and blossomed. She is of average height and shares the battle of excess kilos with many women. When I first met her in 1982, she had only two blouses and two straight skirts, which were not particularly flattering. With a salary of 200 rubles a month, she could afford nothing more. I bought clothes for her and introduced her to another style that suited her, and other friends encouraged her to style her hair and to wear makeup. Larissa tinted her hair chestnut and had it cut short and layered, which made her look younger and not quite so serious. She also used eye shadow, which made her pale blue eyes stand out. The new Larissa, with her Western look, was quite attractive. But her mother had another opinion, Larissa said. Valentina criticized her daughter's jeans and long skirts, saying they made her look suspiciously like a hooligan or gypsy.

When Valentina made one of her rare trips to Moscow to visit Larissa I asked to meet her but came up against vehement opposition. Larissa was proud of her two half sisters, whom she wanted me to meet, but not of her mother, who was an embarrassment. "She talks like a sewing machine. She can be aggressive. She should take tranquilizers but refuses." I persisted, and Larissa finally agreed to drop her off at my flat.

A short, gray-haired woman, who looked younger than her sixty-seven years, greeted me with a broad smile that showed her silver teeth. It was a warm summer day and Valentina was wearing a red suit that a foreign friend had given Larissa fifteen years ago, when minis were in fashion. The rows of medals on her jacket attracted my attention at once. I had never had a distinguished veteran of the Second World War as a guest in my apartment. She had been awarded this honor for singing in a cultural brigade at the front, she said proudly.

Larissa strongly opposed Valentina wearing her medals in Moscow, explaining that they should be worn only on holidays. "Coming to Moscow is a holiday for me," her mother said. "And why shouldn't I wear them? I am not a drunk, prostitute, or thief. I am proud of my medals, which I earned honestly." She also did not want to risk leaving her medals at home where they might be stolen.

She seemed to feel completely at home within minutes. She took off her jacket, revealing a good figure, unbuttoned her blouse, and took off her shoes, exposing bunions that were covered with adhesive tape. For the next two hours I played hostess and Valentina talked. It was not always easy to follow her conversation. She jumped from one subject to the next, and I sometimes lagged behind. When she wanted to make a point, which was often, she would stab her finger in the air and become loud and excited.

Larissa's mother's first recollection of the Germans was in 1943 when she tasted German bread and ham. Somehow that memory reminded her of the letter she had written as a child to Stalin, telling him how much she loved him. Now she was receiving a pension of almost 85 rubles a month, which was just enough to buy staples and cover the cost of an apartment. Valentina had a sensitive stomach and could not eat fatty or spicy foods. Thank goodness Larissa sent her food packages from Moscow, she said. Honey, tea, olive oil, and canned goods agreed with her stomach.

Her physical problems did not end with her stomach. After listing her other ailments, she said that medicine used to be free of charge, but now there was a charge, and it cost more than she could afford. When she talked about how children should be brought up, I recalled Larissa's anger at her mother's letters, which she threw away unopened. It was her grandmother's philosophical letters, with spelling errors, that Larissa cherished.

Just before Larissa's mother departed she said, "My daughter was reluctant to introduce me to you because you are an aristocrat and who am I?" This remark touched me, and I embraced her. "You are always welcome," I assured her. I liked her self-confidence and frankness, but her constant chatter and unreflective judgments would have gotten on my nerves after a while. I understood Larissa's attitude toward her mother a little better after that visit.

Natasha was the next family member who came to visit. She was Larissa's half sister and was ten years younger. They bore no physical likeness to one another even though they had the same mother. Natasha was petite and weighed no more than 45 kilos. Her exact height was the subject of serious discussion. She had read in her favorite journal, and verified elsewhere, that people shrink by 2 centimeters during the day. Since we met in the morning, she was at her greatest height, 164 centimeters [5 feet 4 inches]. The color of her eyes was also disputable. They were black when she was young, but now she maintained that they were light brown, although I saw grayish-green eyes staring from behind untinted glasses. Short, brown hair framed her pretty face with its high cheekbones, small sculptured nose, and flawless skin. Her youthful appearance fooled not only me, but her students. When she entered her classroom for the first time, students thought she was a classmate.

Natasha, like Larissa, spent a happy and carefree childhood with her grandmother, who encouraged her to read and spoiled her. In a giggling, embarrassed voice she admitted that her grandmother washed her clothing and even her hair until she was fifteen. When Natasha finished school, Larissa encouraged her sister to join her in Moscow to study. It took her five years to pass the entrance exams at Moscow University. She said that had she been a party member or from an influential family, she would have been admitted at once. While she waited to be accepted at the university, she delivered mail in her hometown and worked in a Moscow tire factory. Her first years in Moscow were difficult because she was a limitchik—one who accepts a menial job in Moscow in order to earn the right to live in the city permanently. She had to share a filthy, drafty room with drunks, prostitutes, and screaming children.

Like Larissa, Natasha earned a Ph.D. in philosophy. She was then assigned to teach at an educational institute in the Siberian city of Barnaul, a 58-hour train trip east of Moscow. Former convicts who were not permitted to reside elsewhere in the Soviet Union lived here, and the city was also known as an ecological disaster zone. Natasha inhaled black polluted air and smelled the abominable odor of Barnaul's chemical industry every day. She compared her two-year obligatory teaching assignment there to the two years Lenin was forced to live in exile.

When her term ended, she applied for teaching positions in other cities and finally accepted an offer in Belgorod, a 10-hour train ride south of Moscow. When Natasha was young she wanted to live in Moscow, but while a student there, she found the pace too fast. She remembered the remark a man made who rushed past her during her first days in Moscow. He shouted, "Do you think you are on a promenade?"

"In Belgorod the people move slowly, like cows. When I arrived in 1988 I believed that they thought about nothing, but I was mistaken. It is their form of self-preservation. Not as many interesting people live in Belgorod as in Moscow, but at least they are relaxed and good-natured. Muscovites are too materialistic, aggressive, and rude," she said, and then covered her mouth in embarrassment and mumbled apologetically, "I really should not have made such an offensive remark."

A few years ago Natasha came to Moscow to buy food supplies. Now she brought food from Belgorod to Moscow when Moscow shops were practically empty and the Belgorod shops still sold milk, meat, and sour cream daily. "How long are the queues?" I asked. "The queues are short compared to those in Moscow, but Belgorod only has 300,000 residents," she said.

Had she noticed any changes in Belgorod during the past few years? Tiny Belgorod used to be a peaceful city, free of conflicts between nationalities, she said. The arrival of 30,000 refugees since 1990 has changed the situation. Meskhetian Turks and Armenians, who were driven from the republics where they lived in the minority, settled on the outskirts of Belgorod. When Natasha's Uzbek students heard rumors that Meskhetian Turks had killed some of their countrymen in Uzbekistan, they sought revenge by beating up and knifing some of the refugees. The local residents, ethnic Russians, were incensed that these strangers had interrupted their peace and wanted them expelled.

Speaking in her high-pitched voice, Natasha continued, "Belgorod residents have also become more uneasy." At the beginning of glasnost they were glued to their televisions and snapped up newspapers. Everything was so new and exciting, but then the changes and bad news began to disturb their calm, stable existence. "Every day we were confronted with another terrible event," Natasha said, listing disquieting scenes shown on national television in 1990 and 1991: weapons being confiscated from civilians in Armenia, violence between nationalities, street crime and the Mafia, food left to rot on trains, striking miners threatening not to send coal to Moscow, a plague epidemic in the north, three airplanes hijacked by citizens seeking asylum abroad, and tobacco stands and cars vandalized because of the cigarette shortage.

The citizens of Belgorod began to regard glasnost as "verbal irresponsibility" and read fewer newspapers and watched less television. They had been living in a peaceful cocoon, isolated from the bitter truths of their own world and the world outside. Glasnost lifted the Iron Curtain and the public finally got a realistic picture of the West, which had been distorted by propaganda. "They know that their life has been bad and is getting worse, but they have reached a saturation point. They are only interested in what happens to them on the streets, at work, and at home. Inflation, crime, and eventual unemployment are their main concerns. They do not understand that these are the results of a national catastrophe and not the cause. They believe that the president should decree that prices stabilize, and then they will be satisfied," Natasha said.

"People in the provinces are not as informed about politics, or even as interested, as Muscovites," she said. "When I explained the meaning of totalitarianism to my students, they asked, 'Why is it bad and why is democracy good?' They do not have basic ethical or moral values. For example, they do not understand why it is wrong to beat a child, if everyone else does it," she said.

A Russian friend, who was widely traveled, brought the discussion of good and bad down to a practical level. "We have no opportunity to compare," he began. "We have been isolated from the outside world for many years." He used the simple example of Soviet waiters, who are notorious for their rudeness, indifference, and poor service. "A waiter might be intelligent, but how can he know what it means to be a good waiter without being shown how good waiters work? The same applies to manners on the streets, in buses, in shops, at the table."

"For more than seventy years we have heard the same propaganda, have been told how to think, and what to believe. Why should a person have to think if he is used to having somebody else think for him and tell him what is right and wrong? Your history begins with the birth of Christ, and ours with the birth of Lenin. Everything that we once considered good, such as the revolution and Lenin, is now bad. Capitalism used to be bad, now it is good."

"We have deposed our idols, such as God, the Czar, Lenin, and Stalin and have not replaced them. We must have someone to worship, and Gorbachev is not the right man. He is like a fighter who puts up his fists to fight and then doesn't fight. The masses know that Stalin was a terrible man, but they say, at least he gave us something to eat, smoke, and drink. Gorbachev may be a good man, but he has not given us anything but empty shops."

"At this moment we know what is bad, but not what is good. Communism used to be our future, but we had no idea what that meant, except in theoretical terms. If you don't know where you are going and what you will experience there, you won't be in a hurry."

This reminded him of a joke that summed up the situation in 1988. "A train was clacking along, but suddenly the tracks ended. How did Lenin solve the problem? He said we must cut down trees and use them for tracks. Stalin favored killing people and using their bodies for tracks. My friend forgot what Khrushchev's solution was, but remembered that Brezhnev closed the train's curtains and rocked back and forth so the people thought the train was moving. Gorbachev asked the passengers to do something, but it was the time of glasnost and they only hung their heads out of the window and shouted angrily, 'Why is the train not moving? Who is guilty?' Today the majority shouts and criticizes but does nothing to try to solve the problems."

"How have your students reacted to the changes Gorbachev introduced?" I asked Natasha. "All the events that have taken place in the country hardly affect them." In one lecture she explained democracy to her class. "This is a social process in which everyone, without exception, should participate," she said. "What can we do?" a student asked. Natasha responded, "You can change what you don't like in Belgorod." "But everything is forbidden and we won't receive permission," he responded. "Then you have to fight for your rights," she said. "The young people are treated like domestic animals here," she told me. "They are fed and taken care of. They are on a leash and wear a muzzle. They feel that they have no right to voice their opinion, and therefore, they have no opinion."

Unlike her students, Natasha was not afraid to voice her opinion and gave me an example of how she defended her rights. Her teaching institute had an opportunity to send teachers to the United States for a special course, and she asked the director if she could apply. This man had Natasha write articles that he passed off as his and he received the praise and the honoraria. "It's not that easy," he told her. "You must give me a part of the stipend and disclaim the right to your salary at this institute while abroad." "But it is a business trip," Natasha said indignantly, "and I am entitled to receive my salary." "The administration understands this, but a teaching position is left empty at the institute, and we must pay for a substitute." Natasha declared her willingness to give up a part of her stipend, but at the same time she told him that it was illegal and that she could take him to court. She was so angry that she threatened to give an interview to Radio Free Europe. This left him speechless and he sent her out of his office.

"The good times have ended for Communist party members," Natasha said, gloating. "They are no longer invited abroad as paid guests of other Communist parties because the party is practically bankrupt. If I had agreed to give my boss the bribe and the dollar part of my stipend he would have used it for his travels in Western countries."

I was familiar with the humiliating money problems Russian friends had who had gone abroad. The ruble was not convertible, and the amount of foreign currency they could legally change at home was so little that many bought foreign currency on the black market at an astronomical rate of exchange. If they didn't do this they would be forced to live like paupers in the West. That is why some smuggled popular Russian goods, such as caviar, vodka, and lacquered Palekh boxes, to the West; they hoped to sell them in order to earn a little foreign currency.

Foreign currency also plays an important role in Soviet cities that foreign tourists visit and where Beriozka shops are located. In Moscow dollars can buy an enterprising Russian luxuries such as apartments, dachas, and cars. This is not yet the case in Belgorod, other small cities, or the countryside where people exchange goods for services.

After discovering that rubles could not buy her what she needed, Natasha learned to barter. She had been living with a roommate in a tiny room in a run-down dormitory for three years and had no prospect of having an apartment of her own in the near future. Being practical, she bought a piece of land and planned to build her own dacha. Since building material was scarce, she was required to have written permission to buy bricks. After receiving the permission, she confidently went to the director of a brick factory. He maintained that he didn't have any bricks. "You must have bricks. The head of the brick factories in this district gave me this permission," she said. "If you think that this piece of paper means we have bricks, you are mistaken," he said.

Natasha visited the director every month, and the conversation was the same. "Good morning, Victor Andreevich. I am here again. You know that I am building a dacha and need bricks." And his answer remained the same. "Many brick factories are now being renovated. You know that this material is very much in demand, and we don't have any surplus."

Natasha was so frustrated that she went to Moscow to discuss the problem with her older and more experienced sister. Larissa suggested that she bribe him and gave her Marlboro cigarettes, which were not available in Belgorod. Natasha accepted them gratefully, but then was afraid to go to the director, cigarettes in hand. She worried about the repercussions of a bribe. Finally she decided to risk it. She found the factory director alone in his office and put two packages of Marlboros and a butane lighter on his desk. To her relief his eyes lit up, and he said excitedly, "You can come tomorrow and pick up the bricks."

The next day, Saturday, was normally a day when the factory was closed. Natasha thought that he was doing her a special favor; however, when she arrived she was surprised to see many drivers waiting to load their trucks, so she went to the end of the line.

The director of the factory came up to her unexpectedly and apologized for not recognizing her sooner. His son, who was a student at her institute and was also waiting to pick up bricks, had seen her and told his father. Then she recalled a remark the director had made when she gave him the cigarettes: "I am an old man and don't smoke. The cigarettes are for my son." After giving her the bricks, he whispered, "If you have another chance can you bring me a few more packs?" Before Natasha continued her story, she interrupted herself to comment, "The more important the boss is, the more he needs in order to bribe others to help his children secure good positions."

When Natasha asked for another shipment of bricks she was told that high party functionaries had reserved all surplus bricks for themselves. "They were anticipating being removed from office, and they wanted to build dachas as quickly as possible to guarantee a comfortable life in retirement. And," Natasha said, "they chose the best locations in the district."

The next problem was to get wood for building. To barter for this she would need yeast, she was told, since people who made *samogon,* "homemade vodka," needed yeast.

Natasha's life has become more difficult since perestroika, but she is accustomed to hardship. Her happiness comes from her students, who respect her, and her fertile plot of land, which is her security for the future.

Larissa's professional path led in a different direction from her sister's. "Perestroika gave me the entire world," she said, in her melodic voice. "I have found a niche outside of the official structure and can earn more and live better." Before perestroika she supplemented her small income by knitting gloves, scarves, and sweaters for Russian friends and doing German-Russian translations. Now she can publish her articles in independent publications in Moscow, participate in Austrian and German radio and television programs, and attend seminars abroad.

The first 600 marks she earned for giving a lecture in Germany "changed my life," she said. Unlike other Russians who spent their foreign currency first on clothing and then on electronics, she wasted her "fortune" on food.

Larissa is a wonderful storyteller, and she dramatically related how she made this decision. "After putting the money aside for weeks, a day arrived when my refrigerator was absolutely empty, and I was starving for meat. Either I would have to rise at 6 A.M. in order to reach the private market before the meat was sold out, and then spend the rest of the day lining up to buy other products, or I could shop in the civilized Beriozka world." Because she was used to working late at night and rising mid-morning, the decision was clear. Her last argument was, "I am forty-five years old and have another twenty years to live, if I'm lucky. I can't build a palace out of glass and aluminum with my 600 marks. It would be nice to feel like a normal person and not be pushed, humiliated, or insulted."

I had often heard the expressions "live like a normal person" or "lead a normal life," and I asked what they meant. "It depends on the person. My fifty-year-old neighbor will regard life as normal when she receives a one-room apartment of her own and has enough to eat," Larissa said.

Her friend Irina would consider life normal when she knew that she could feed her children the next day. "My half sister Rita, who is thirteen years younger than I, leads a normal life. She has two children and a devoted husband, who is a biochemist. Together they earn 400 rubles a month. She is the only member of my family with an apartment of her own."

"I have never regarded a life of standing in queues and being humiliated as normal," said Larissa. This led her to recount an unpleasant experience she had in a fish shop in her neighborhood. She loves fish and is even willing to stand in a long line to buy it. While waiting, she felt sick and vomited. Instead of receiving help or sympathy, the other people in line ridiculed her. "You shouldn't come into such a shop if you are pregnant," one woman said. "I'm not pregnant. It's the obnoxious smell. The saleswoman should clean the shop more often," she said. "Show me a fish shop where the smell is different," the clerk replied, and everyone agreed.

"People accept everything here as normal, but I don't," Larissa said. For example, she considered it abnormal to earn only 200 rubles a month after eight years of study and a Ph.D. "I can't be promoted because the older employees refuse to retire and give up their positions to my generation," she said.

One of the benefits of perestroika that has led to a more normal life for Larissa, according to her definition, has been open access to formerly "closed publications." Before perestroika some journals, magazines, and papers could be read only in "the prison for books," the nickname Larissa and her colleagues had given the room where such publications had been available only to a select few. She was also proud that her translation of German philosopher Ernst Bloch into Russian was among works now being published.

Perestroika also gives Larissa the opportunity to travel abroad and earn foreign currency for her lectures and other public appearances. This money will eventually be the down payment for an apartment of her own, a wish she has had her whole life.

I knew how difficult it was to exist in the Soviet Union solely from the official salary one earns, which is why many people had a second income, one that was often considered illegal according to Soviet law. I praised Larissa for what I considered her legal earnings, but she refuted my point. "Your government may have considered this legal, but mine did not. Until now there were no laws to legalize my kind of work. I paid the German and Austrian governments taxes on my earnings, but not my government. Why should I pay taxes to the party leadership? I remember when Brezhnev used our foreign currency to buy foreign cars for himself. I would like to have the legal right to earn foreign currency and to spend it the way I choose whether in my country or abroad."

Larissa was grateful for the future that perestroika had given her, but she felt guilty that she could do so little for her country. She compared her situation to that of a lover whose love is unrequited. "When a woman is in love, she does everything to please her lover, but she cannot force him to love her. She also has no right to condemn him or be angry with him. I am unhappy and disappointed because I have given my love, energy, and talent to my country, and it doesn't seem to need it. Perestroika has given a talented group of young people the chance to prove themselves and to earn high salaries. At the same time the government has created new obstacles, such as oppressive tax laws, to kill their initiative."

"The real fighters for perestroika are the intellectuals who will soon be pensioners. They were active during the 1960s when there was hope for change," she said. "During the 1970s and 1980s they went underground, emigrated, or became alcoholics. It is remarkable that these people, who lost everything, have the energy and vision once again to fight."

Larissa pointed out that today's youth are different. She said that many are cynical and lack ideals and political ambitions. "They have one goal, to live well. For my generation, that was considered immoral."

I have noticed that youth have become enchanted with Western values and capitalism, and they try to bring the Western consumer paradise to their Russian world. This includes an apartment full of imported items such as VCRs, videos, clothes, and cars. What worries me most is their willingness to use almost any means to achieve their end.

"People of my generation are more passive compared to those in their sixties. We want to preserve morality and ethics in a system that does not esteem these values," said Larissa. "Today each person has methods to survive in a world where the law of the jungle rules. I have my work, and this is my only hope."

4

MASHA AND
THE FORGOTTEN

*M*y Russian friends seldom came to visit me empty-handed, and often their gifts were conversation pieces. The eye-catcher was a tea cozy shaped like a rooster fashionably dressed in an Easter bonnet and a frilled skirt, decorated with red and blue papier-mâché flowers. I wanted to order more for friends, and that is how I met Masha, the tea cozy's designer.

One day a friend brought Masha to my apartment. I was delighted to welcome this talented, pretty, twenty-three-year-old girl to my flat. Over the next few hours she sat on the edge of a chair, a frozen smile on her face. She was so shy that she hardly touched her food and said little. When my friend left us alone for a short time, Masha's cheeks flushed and beads of perspiration broke out on her forehead; I was forced to conduct a monologue. This meeting led to many others, but the next ones took place in her home, where her fear of a foreigner disappeared and she had less difficulty talking.

On my first visit to Masha's flat she and her mother greeted me at the door, and I was struck by their physical similarities: Both had long, broad noses turned up slightly at the tip, wide cheekbones, strong jutting chins, and dark warm eyes. Masha, however, was tall and trim, while her mother was short and had filled out over the years. Her tired eyes and pensive expression indicated that her life had not been easy.

The three-room flat that Masha shared with her parents and grandfather was immaculate. Later she admitted that she had spent two days cleaning it up for my arrival. The dining table, located in the large main room in which Masha lived, was set indicating that I would be received there. When my status changed from that of a guest to that of a friend, I could at last sit in their cozy kitchen that was full of plants, homemade preserves, and Masha's wall hangings.

Masha's mother apologized for the modest choice of dishes for tea, but I assured her that homemade blini, marmalade, cabbage pie, and apple cake were my favorites. To prove my point I had seconds of everything. She was relieved to hear that I seldom ate meat, especially because there was a shortage of meat and sausage in the shops. She and Masha were vegetarians, she said, so the shortage did not affect them.

When I praised the delicious strawberry jam, Masha paused for a split second and then said her grandmother had made it shortly before her death, a few months before. A drunken ambulance driver had run over her and a friend at a pedestrian crossing. They were both killed. After the accident, the police questioned the driver and then released him.

I had an uneasy feeling about eating the last jar of jam the grandmother had made, but I could not refuse the additional serving Masha heaped on my blini. "I miss my grandmother very much," she said, almost in a whisper. "She was a kind woman who never offended a soul. She helped everyone. She was very much like my mother."

Masha's mother interrupted: "No, I am stricter." Then she let her daughter continue. "Granny loved spring and summer and used to talk to the flowers. She watered our pitiful Moscow trees that grow in filthy, polluted surroundings." After a long silence she said, as a few tears trickled down her cheeks, "I always dreamed of presenting my grandmother with a special gift, and I finally found an extraordinary shawl, but she died before I could give it to her."

Masha was brought up by her grandmother in surroundings that encouraged her creativity. "Granny used to say that a child is supposed to have beautiful toys in order to distinguish between what is pretty and what is ugly. I always had wonderful dolls and made gowns for them out of old clothes."

Once, when she was shopping with her grandmother, an artist stopped them and asked permission to paint their portraits because they looked so much alike. Masha began to visit the artist regularly. Sometimes her mother came along, and Masha would paint her mother while the artist painted her. The artist predicted that Masha would be an artist, and her prediction came true.

Masha loved nature and spent summer holidays with her grandmother in a small village; she painted from morning until night. She wanted to paint the sea but when she finally saw it, she cried. "It was not what I had imagined. The weather was overcast, and weeds made the shallow water look green. Some years later I visited the Black Sea, and then I could paint the sea of my dreams," she said.

Masha's interest in art was evident in every nook and cranny of her room. Rolls of paper and boxes of paints bought over the past few years when these items were available were on top of her closet and in corners of the room. She pointed to a pastel on the wall, whose asymmetric shapes and harmonious colors had already attracted my attention, and said it was her favorite. It was mine also, but I did not dare tell her because I knew she would have given it to me immediately.

She could sew everything from theater costumes that she had designed to gold-stitched embroidery for church altars. "Now I have a problem finding fabrics and sewing material," she said. "A year ago the shops were full, but now most are empty or closed."

In 1991 the vice minister in the Ministry of Commerce confirmed this fact and prepared people for even harder times. "The stock of consumer goods is dwindling rapidly and is almost exhausted," he said. He compared 1989 production figures to 1990 figures, which showed dramatically fewer consumer goods available in January and February 1991. As an example he cited the shoe industry, whose 1990 production of 23 million pairs of shoes could cover only one-third of consumers' needs. He also listed other losses during this period: 100 million pairs of stockings, 30,000 tons of soap, 110,000 vacuum cleaners, and 70,000 washing machines.

I had heard a number of explanations for the shortages, and all seemed plausible. *Pravda*, the party's daily newspaper, reprimanded consumers for not behaving reasonably, maintaining that the Soviet economy could provide the basics for the people if they did not hoard. It was clear to me that people would behave reasonably only if they were confident that the shelves would be full each day. Another explanation was that factories were selling their products abroad for foreign currency.

Economists, meanwhile, wrote about the inefficiency of the system, and many people attributed shortages to a "blockade" of Moscow. In the past, centralized planning compelled cities to send their products to Moscow, and their residents then had to come to Moscow to buy what was produced in their hometowns. New regulations enacted in 1989 prevented non-Muscovites from shopping in Moscow. Cities that had once supplied Moscow now held goods back for their own residents.

Politics also played a significant role. Conservative party functionaries, whose positions were threatened by strong democratic forces in Moscow and in cities such as Leningrad and Sverdlovsk, apparently wanted to create discontent in the population so that the democrats would lose power. They tried, it seemed, to starve these cities, and "sabotage" was the word most often used to describe their tactics.

Shocking television programs showed the flagrant destruction of food. Friends told me about having seen containers filled with rotting sausage; a journalist told me about a radio appeal for people to help unload food from trains. When students arrived, an unidentified person, he said, allegedly paid each 50 rubles to go home. A friend's brother worked in potato fields so that he could receive his salary in potatoes; he was stopped on his way home by men armed with machine guns who confiscated his potatoes and burned them in front of him.

Everyone blamed the Mafia, and arrests shown on television indicated that factory workers and working-class gangs were the criminals. This was only part of the truth. The government's inability to enforce law and order was an indication to my friends and to me that the real Mafia was working in the ministries, KGB, and central government.

Die Zeit magazine (May 10, 1991), in an exposé of the Mafia, confirmed this point. A Soviet source was quoted as saying, "Gorbachev's party does not work against the Mafia; it works with the Mafia. The *nomenklatura* and the state machinery are a part of this organization. The Mafia is an instrument for retaining power."

The same article quoted a KGB examining magistrate: "I even received orders from superiors to stop an investigation because big shots in the Communist party were involved."

In the well-known liberal Soviet magazine *Literaturnaya gazeta,* Anatoly Rubinov was even bolder. The popular Russian author wrote, "In the Soviet Union ... the party is the real Mafia and it supports organized crime. The Ministry of the Interior blames the Mafia in order to hide its own mistakes."

Needy groups, such as the working class, invalids, divorced mothers, pensioners, and young married couples, were not particularly interested in who was to blame for the food and clothing shortages, because they could not do anything about them. They were simply victims like Masha's friend Vera, who stopped by and talked about her dreary everyday life. She was married, had a six-year-old son, and worked because her family could not live on her husband's salary alone. The best part of her job at a fur factory was the opportunity to order scarce products. "Sometimes the employees receive noodles, meat, or even special cookies and candy," she said. "I don't have time to stand in line for three hours to buy food."

At night she studied at the art institute with Masha and got home at 10:30 P.M. "I don't have a minute to myself, and I can find time for my son only on weekends," she said. She was so keyed up that I did not dare interrupt. "I am pessimistic about the future and don't want to talk politics. But we cannot rely on our present government to enact measures that will improve our standard of living. When I was a schoolgirl I wondered why people in the West accused my government of violating human rights. Back then I believed that everyone here was free and that no one was oppressed. In the seventh grade I finally understood that our kind of society, although it may be called 'socialism,' is unjust. Some people enjoy all of the privileges at the expense of others. We have never lived in a democracy and don't know what freedom and democracy mean. My son, for example, asked my husband, 'Who is more important, the president or a militia man?' He answered, 'The president, because of his position.' The truth is the militia man, who wields his authority in the theaters and museums, in shops and restaurants, on the streets, in the subway stations ..."

After Vera rushed off to work, Masha's mother reminisced about her daughter's childhood. She could not forget the day she came home from work to find smoke pouring out of a window of their flat. She dashed into the apartment to find Masha quietly baking clay in the oven. The ram Masha had been modeling on that day was placed on a beautiful antique piano at the other end of the room. I wanted to see the ram up close as well as the piano and other antiques in the room. I walked to the piano, which had a plaque that was inscribed with the maker's name: Max Adam—Berlin. On either side of the plaque were two brass candlesticks, which stood out from the piano. The piano and a tall ornamental commode had belonged to her grandmother, Masha said. Masha's bed, covered with her favorite stuffed animals from her childhood, stood between the two antiques. The woven carpet behind her bed was one of the few wall hangings that her golden hands had not created.

Beginning in the eighth grade Masha dreamed of attending art school, her mother said, but "my husband and I were only simple workers, who knew no influential people. We also did not have money for a tutor, and so I decided to coach her in Russian, her weakest subject. The happiest day of my life was when Masha passed the entrance exams. God took her hand." When Masha's mother made this remark, she smiled for the first time, a radiant smile that brightened her otherwise sad face.

Masha's evening studies at the art institute and daytime job in a textile factory left her little free time, and if she had a few spare hours she did not spend them discussing politics, as she and her friends had done in the past. "When Gorbachev first took office he gave us reason to believe in something, but now ... We have been hearing the same words and promises for years, but nothing has changed for the better," Masha said.

"I do not believe anyone anymore," her mother said. "There is no hope unless the party confesses its sins and corrects the injustices of the system. It must change its course completely." She then told me about herself. When she was younger she skied and climbed mountains, visited museums, and went to the theater. She even took a course in yoga. Pointing to the books on the shelves, she said, "I used to read, but now I have no time. I also was cheerful and gregarious, but ... It is impossible to live when every day is worse than the one before. I have worked hard my whole life, and now, just before retirement, I am afraid of what tomorrow will bring. The church is the only place that gives me strength to face the next day."

Masha's mother was particularly bitter about an event that had taken place in Moscow in March 1991. The central Soviet government issued a three-week ban against rallies in the capital. The leadership claimed that democratic forces were "unleashing shameless anti-Communist propaganda" and creating an "atmosphere of terror" against party members. The ban was to be in effect when the parliament of the Russian Republic was scheduled to decide the fate of Boris Yeltsin, its president. A minority of hard-line Communists wanted him ousted, and they claimed that rallies would intimidate them and interfere with their legislative duties. They opposed Yeltsin mainly because of his demand that Gorbachev resign and they were enraged by Yeltsin's support of the Baltic republics' quest for autonomy and his proposal for a separate Russian army.

To ensure the ban's enforcement, President Gorbachev took police powers from the Moscow city council and turned them over to the Ministry of the Interior. Prime Minister Valentin Pavlov fueled the fire by alluding to "looming threats." The deputy editor of *Pravda* wrote, "Preparations for the final storming of the Kremlin have already begun." *Pravda* also warned potential demonstrators who might break the ban not to be used as marionettes by the "power hungry democrats," whom the newspaper referred to as criminals.

The Moscow city government, with its democratic majority, voted almost two to one to overrule Gorbachev's decree forbidding public demonstrations and gave permission for the rally. Gavril Popov, the mayor of Moscow, defended the decision, saying, "Those who accuse us have actually chosen a confrontational course and are trying to bring it to life." He pointed out that not a single violent incident had taken place during a demonstration in Moscow for the past two years.

On March 28, the day the rallies and demonstrations were to take place, Masha and her mother headed for the center of the city. They passed troops in riot gear on their way. Militia and soldiers who lined the streets tried to stop them, but Masha's mother was determined. They had to show their passports at every checkpoint and they were asked where they were going. Masha's mother gave the address of a friend who lived in the city center. They were allowed to pass while others were turned back. All streets to the Kremlin were sealed off by an army of trucks, a water cannon, and an officially estimated force of 50,000 police, Interior Ministry troops, and soldiers.

Masha and her mother joined the thousands who were walking down the main street that encircles the center of the capital. Some of the demonstrators carried posters with the plea "Gorbachev resign," and others with "Save Russia from the Communist party." They often shouted Yeltsin's name and admonished the troops with the words, "Shame, shame."

Moscow city council deputies and Russian Republic deputies adjourned their sessions in order to participate in the rallies and demonstrations. They took positions at the front end of the column in order to protect demonstrators from any possible attack by the security forces.

The next day *Izvestia,* the government newspaper, published that the decision to use troops to stop the march "cast shame on the authorities." While part of the Soviet press was critical, the state-run television refrained from any coverage of the banned demonstration.

"I will never forget that awful day," Masha said. "Rows of policemen, trucks, and soldiers were everywhere. The special militia wore helmets and bullet-proof vests. Since Gorbachev had forbidden weapons, the soldiers were equipped with tear gas and clubs. The troops looked as though they were ready to fight. I don't understand why this was necessary in such a peaceful city."

In spite of predictions that March 28 could be a bloodbath like the one on Tiananmen Square in Beijing in June 1989, the day ended peacefully and was a great victory for the democratic forces. The head of the extreme democratic wing, Nikolai Travkin, said, "We have crossed the threshold of fear. The government can no longer use force to intimidate the people to obey." One of the popular independent Soviet newspapers described the event as "Gorbachev's Waterloo." "The gunslinger has no more bullets," it commented. This was the first time that hundreds of thousands of Muscovites had defied a government ban and won. While the authority of the central government was diminishing, Yeltsin's popularity was growing.

Masha's mother explained that she had joined the demonstrators on March 28 because she wanted to teach her daughter a lesson so that she would fight for her rights in the future. "Young people must be politically active in order to put an end to the injustices and indignities that I have experienced my whole life," she said. "I have never been treated like a human being, and I also have no rights. I am not even allowed to move to another town to find work without overcoming all kinds of obstacles. This system chains us like slaves."

"I agree with Mama," Masha said. She would be graduating from the art institute soon, but was not certain if she would be able to find a position in her field. Her dream was to design theater costumes, but she said she didn't know any artists or people "who can help me." She and other talented classmates would have liked to open a workshop to sell their handicrafts privately, but this required material and equipment. It was also risky, she said. She talked about a friend who sold his paintings in the Arbat, a famous old quarter in the center of Moscow. He had to pay money to the militia man who patrolled the street, to the racketeers who demanded protection money, and to a person who stored his paintings. If he refused he would have been beaten up and his paintings destroyed.

Her mother commented, "A state is doomed when it permits black marketeers, the Mafia, and speculators to live better and have more opportunities than those with talent." Masha's mother was speaking from her own bitter experience. She had graduated from a construction and engineering institute, and her first job had been with an architectural organization. Her idealism and enthusiasm made her even forget that she earned only a pittance. She soon realized that no one was interested in her innovative ideas or ability and that she would be better off if she acted like some of her colleagues who drank tea or busied themselves most of the day earning income from other sources. Her disappointment with her job and a move to a new flat in another district of Moscow gave her reason to look for other work. The only job she could find was as a cleaning woman in a hotel, and it paid a monthly wage of 140 rubles.

Jointly, Masha and her parents brought home less than 400 rubles a month, enough to cover their basic needs until prices rose on April 2, 1991. They had always lived modestly, but now they had to struggle to make ends meet. The price of meat went from 2 rubles to 7 rubles a kilo, one egg from 13 to 26 kopecks, a liter of milk from 28 to 50 kopecks, and butter from 3.60 rubles to more than 8 rubles a kilo. The price of salt rose 240 percent, sugar 135 percent, tea, oil, and cigarettes 100 percent, children's clothing 130 percent, train tickets 70 percent, and airline tickets 80 percent. The increase in the cost of public transportation was a particularly hard blow. A monthly bus, subway, and tram ticket now cost 18 rubles instead of 6. To compensate for the officially estimated increase in living costs of more than 70 percent, the government promised to give every working person an additional 60 rubles per month and pensioners an additional 65, but everyone knew that this would not come close to covering the increased cost of living.

The reason Gorbachev gave for making "one of the most unpopular decisions since he came to power in 1985," *Tass,* the official press agency, reported, was to avoid an economic collapse in the country. Economists agreed that a decision to end state subsidies and move toward a free-market system was long overdue, but they said, according to the April 12, 1991, *New York Times,* that "there was little chance that the increased prices alone would stimulate any more production." They painted a gloomy picture of the country's economic situation, including a decrease in investments, instability, a huge foreign debt, the loss of long-term foreign credit, and the collapse of internal economic ties.

Masha's mother understood economics only in terms of how it affected her life. No doubt she was thinking of Masha when she said, "I don't know how young couples with children will manage in the future. A dress for a little girl costs 80 rubles, a pair of shoes 50. The children's breakfast that used to cost 20 kopecks now costs 60, and lunch almost 2 rubles. School uniforms for the first grade cost 62 rubles. There is no baby food and kindergartens have no room for more children." Masha interrupted to say, "If I were married I could not afford to bring up a child today."

Masha was one of the few in her age group who was still single. She had a boyfriend but was reluctant to marry, she said, because she did not want to have a marriage like her parents. She did not elaborate, but mentioned that her father was a difficult person. "He treated Grandmother badly when she was alive, and he does not talk to my grandfather today."

Her expressive face told me that it was time to change the subject, and I asked, "Do you have a dream?" This question took her by surprise and while she thought, she twisted a curl of her wavy shoulder-length hair around her finger. Finally she said breathlessly, almost as though she were afraid to express the thought, "I want to visit foreign countries." Then she looked down and said, almost in a whisper, "I know this will not be possible because we are poor." I told her that she could earn a little money on her own for such a trip, and she looked at me, baffled. Until then she had given her handiwork away as gifts; now I volunteered to show her work to friends.

I returned to Germany with a suitcase full of Masha's original creations and started taking orders from many friends who were as impressed with her talent as I. Within a few weeks she had many sponsors who sent her a new sewing machine, needles, threads, and material. If her own country would not recognize and encourage her talent, at least we could give her a chance. Masha became a model for a new kind of aid to the former Soviet Union. I call it "help people to help themselves."

Masha was young, healthy, and still idealistic. She had a life to look forward to, while many others could only expect more difficult times. During the winter of 1990 and 1991, when Germans sent more than 1 billion marks of assistance to the Soviet Union to help the poor and forgotten survive a period of food shortages, I met pensioners who were in such desperate straits that they could only look forward to death.

One of these pensioners lived in a run-down building located on Gorbachev's daily route to work. When I entered the building, my first thoughts were that it was a firetrap and that no one should be permitted to live here. I became angry at the government's disregard for its people and the indignities to which they were subjected.

I was with my friend Masha, the adventurer, who had the apartment number of the pensioner, an eighty-year-old woman, whose package we wanted to deliver. Masha was one of my Russian friends who had become active in distributing German help to the needy. When we stood in front of the building we were confronted with a row of seven bells and no names. This meant that seven families shared a communal flat. I pressed the first bell and worked my way down the row until I heard the sound of shuffling feet approaching the door. "She is almost blind and needs time," Masha said. This pensioner was on the list of poor that Masha had gotten from Moscow city council deputies.

The stale odor of garbage and urine in the building's corridor overwhelmed me when the door opened, and I was afraid I would vomit. I felt better as soon as the woman shut the door to her room. In spite of the closed window the draft was so strong that we kept our coats on. The pensioner was accustomed to the cold and was dressed in layers of clothes that hung on her emaciated body.

This dark, dreary room had been her "home" for fifteen years. The bare floor was scratched and discolored as was the worn-out furniture, but she had the essentials: a bed, table, closet, and cupboard. Her television and refrigerator were in need of repair, she said, but the radio worked. This was her main contact with the outside world, which she no longer entered. She could not even remember when she had last taken a walk on the street.

She was interested in politics, and the commentaries she heard daily on the radio kept her informed. She criticized Gorbachev for the empty stores, but excused him for his mistakes with the remark, "He tore down the Berlin Wall."

The wall of her room documented photographically her aristocratic background. She and her family had lived in a twelve-room mansion until it was confiscated following the revolution in 1917. The photos were the only part of her past that she was able to save. Soon she would be the last of her family, she said. Her brother was dying of cancer, and her other relatives had been shot or had died in prison during the 1930s. Her life had been a series of tragedies, culminating with the death of her only son from a childhood disease.

For the past fifty years she had paid the price for her heritage. Her persecution had begun at the age of twenty when she was arrested and then interrogated for several days in Moscow's notorious Lubyanka prison. "I was forced to sleep on the cold, dirty floor," she said and then continued, as though it had happened only yesterday. "I was wearing a red dress when they picked me up. When I was released the dress was black," she said, wiping away a tear. "The last happy day of my life that I remember was when I was seven years old and went to my last family party," she said.

Her deteriorating eyesight forced her to wear thick glasses that gave her only 10 percent vision in one eye. I noticed the difficulty she had in moving around and asked if her neighbors took care of her. "They drink, curse me, and wish I were dead. Then they would have my room. Not long ago I fell down, and they did not help me. It would have been better if I had died, but God is not ready to relieve me of my misery."

Her doorbell rang, and a teenager walked in carrying a stack of oval aluminum tins. She was from a nearby school that provided meal service five days a week for the homebound. The school kitchen prepared the food and students distributed it. The girl greeted the old woman and emptied the contents of the aluminum tin onto a plate. The pensioner angrily pushed it aside, and I was shocked. I thought she was lucky to receive this individual care, which had been initiated by the students. "Look at this food. No dog would eat it," the pensioner said. The fried, cold, unidentifiable dish looked inedible, but it was not the student's fault.

I praised the girl, who had blushed at the old lady's scolding, for volunteering to help the needy. After the pensioner refused her lunch, Masha and I opened our package and carefully selected only the foods that we thought she would most likely eat. We gave her milk powder, muesli, and cocoa, explaining what each item was and how to prepare it. The mini-chocolate bars pleased her instantly, and her mood seemed to improve as she nibbled away. I regretted that we had so few suitable items for her. If only we had visited her before, then we would have known what she needed. When she mentioned that a young man from a government agency went shopping for her once a week, I was slightly relieved. Otherwise she most likely would have starved to death.

She became frightened at new sounds in the corridor and she asked us to hide everything immediately. Her neighbors occasionally forced their way into her room, roughed her up, and stole things, she said. We quietly left the flat, totally disheartened, and hoped that our visit had not been noticed.

This experience still depresses me because I realize she is only one of the millions who needs help. When we visited the pensioner in winter 1991, the newspapers and magazines were full of letters from desperate mothers. One of these mothers, who lived about two hours from Moscow, wrote, "Every person is permitted to buy 250 grams of oil, 500 grams of sugar, 500 grams of noodles, 80 grams of cream of wheat, 120 grams of rice, 120 grams of grain products per month. How can these amounts satisfy anyone? Who set such standards? When a baby is in the family, it cannot survive on a few spoonfuls of cooked cereal daily. I have three children and I don't know how I can save them from starvation. We do not expect help. My husband and I are wise enough to know that we can only rely on ourselves. Can the government please tell me how children can grow up healthy today?"

Another letter from a mother who lived closer to Moscow read, "My family and I will die out like dinosaurs. We have seven children, and just imagine," she wrote bitterly, "each one wants to eat daily. Everything we can buy in shops is rationed. The amounts do not provide children with enough vitamins. Why do we need perestroika if it brings hunger to children? And now I hear that life will be worse. How can it be worse, when I must feed my one-year-old daughter the same thing every day? Fruit and vegetables cost between 8 and 10 rubles a kilo at the private market. I earn 350 rubles and this must feed nine people. It is winter. The children don't have anything to wear. I have decided not to send them to school. Their present existence is worse than death. Everyone criticizes the 'time of stagnation' (Brezhnev years), but during that time there was enough food. Now the shelves are empty, and that is called perestroika. The government should not ask us to wait. What happens later is not important to me. My children need to eat today. By the time government promises become reality we will be dead. I don't believe in a bright future anymore and do not have any faith in the government."

A sixteen-year-old named Valery wrote to *Komsomolskaya pravda,* a favorite newspaper among young people, that he wanted to commit suicide. He was living in a quagmire and there was no way out. All of the "holy" people he once believed in are now considered bad, he said. He used Lenin as an example and wrote, "Our clean vase has been broken, but we have not been given a new one. If we received one it would have to be made out of plastique so that one could do whatever one wants with it. When people lose their idol they become angry and aggressive. They are able to kill just for fun. I am afraid to live."

Another moving letter was from a mother who wrote, "I have committed a crime. I have brought five children into the world. I work in a factory and cannot afford to give my children meat or fruit. The best I can offer them is carrots. I am afraid of the future. I know if a time comes when the children beg for food, and I cannot give them anything, I will kill them."

These letters, published in winter 1991, were in response to the wave of humanitarian help to the Soviet Union, 80 percent of which came from Germany. This overwhelming German reaction can be attributed to many factors, the most important of which is the Germans' admiration for Gorbachev, which I call "Gorbimania." Chancellor Helmut Kohl also reminded Germans that Gorbachev had helped Germany to reunite and said, "The winter is coming and hunger is threatening Soviet cities and villages. We all should feel responsible and be prepared to help our neighbor." Foreign Minister Hans Dieter Genscher supported this action, which he called "an expression of united European solidarity."

The Russian response to this aid in the Soviet Union varied from gratitude to embarrassment. One woman said, "For seventy-four years we have been told how rich and great we are. Now we are experiencing not only an economic but also a moral crisis. We are still feeding Afghanistan and Cuba. It is difficult for simple people like me to understand why we have been sending billions of rubles of help to others when we are not in the position to feed our own population. I also don't understand how we can spend 20 billion rubles to build a plane while our shops are empty." Another said, "This help has enabled us to understand how inhumane our system is in contrast to the humane systems abroad."

My experience after the December 1988 earthquake in Armenia taught me that there is one kind of help that is guaranteed to arrive in the Soviet Union: It is help that is delivered directly to those who need it or to responsible and honest people who can assure its fair distribution. I call it "door to door" help and advocated this kind of aid in response to the Kohl and Genscher appeal. I organized a team of close friends in Moscow who sent me lists, authorized by Moscow city council deputies, with names, addresses, and the specific needs of the "forgotten," who were in desperate straits. I passed these names on to the Dostoevsky and Door to Door associations in Germany, which recruited volunteers to prepare packages for shipment. The Hanover Red Cross and the Klingenberg shipping firm generously offered to truck everything free of charge.

I was in Moscow when the trucks arrived and I helped my team distribute some of the packages. One of our objectives was to furnish warm clothing and winter boots to the elderly. To make certain that the pensioners got the correct sizes I urged them to try the clothing on at once; if a size was wrong, we had them exchange it for the correct one. I wanted to prevent our clothing from being sold on the black market.

One family of two children, a mother, and grandmother came to my attention because we had forgotten the seventy-year-old grandmother. I arrived at their apartment a few days later with a package of warm clothing and winter boots. The grandmother, surprised by my unannounced visit, was so overwhelmed that she embraced me and burst into tears. I was as moved as she and agreed to stay for a cup of tea.

Her two-room apartment looked as though a hurricane had struck. She apologized for the disorder, but she had been sick and had no time to clean. The tiny kitchen was in such a state that she suggested that we sit in her room at the end of the corridor. I made my way carefully through the obstacle course and passed another untidy room, where her seven-year-old granddaughter was playing.

The grandmother's room was large enough for two single beds, a bursting bookcase, and spacious closet. Her fourteen-year-old granddaughter, whom she introduced as Nadya, was doing her homework at a small desk in a corner. Nadya's long straight blond hair, delicate features, and white velvet skin reminded me of Cinderella.

Our conversation had just begun, when her daughter, Irina, returned from work, pale and exhausted. She joined her mother on the bed; I sat across from them in a roomy armchair. The grandmother was descended from a noble family, like the other old lady I had met, and she also had a tragic history to relate. She and her husband had not registered their marriage, she told me, because her aristocratic heritage might have spoiled his career. Police arrested him in the 1940s for participating in revolutionary activities and her for her aristocratic background. When they were released from prison Khrushchev asked her husband to start a newspaper devoted to economics.

While her mother wiped away tears, Irina said, "Father would turn in his grave today if he knew how the party has destroyed the country. He was a devoted Communist who helped to build the Soviet power." Irina's mother, who usually dominated the conversation, interrupted to tell about her father's attempted flight from the Communists during the revolution. He was killed, but her mother, who lived to age eighty, survived because the servants in their manor protected her.

She revisited her native town in 1975. When she arrived, a woman came up to her and addressed her by name; she was one of the many orphans her mother and father (Irina's grandmother and grandfather) had raised, educated, and provided with a dowry before marrying. "My mother, an aristocrat, had lived in fear most of her life and left the village immediately. She was afraid that if she stayed longer she would be arrested," said the grandmother.

Irina's mother continued her long family epic and talked about her brother, who had run away from home to become a Communist and was later decorated as a military hero. When she saw him in 1937 she warned that there would be a time when Stalin's name would be used to frighten children. He responded, "If you were not my sister, I would shoot you on the spot." Years later, while he was living in a basement, poverty-stricken, he admitted to his sister that she had spoken the truth. "I have only heard lies my whole life," he said, "and have lived in vain." He died shortly after.

Irina had graduated from the linguistics department of prestigious Moscow University and worked at the Gas Institute in the information section. She earned 170 rubles a month, and her mother's pension amounted to 100 rubles. Their meager earnings put them in the category of "Soviet poor"; this category unofficially includes at least one-half of the population and entitled her children to free lunch in school.

In a February 8, 1991, article in the independent, anticommunist newspaper *Kuranty,* a correspondent asked, "Who is responsible for the poverty: the sick economy, lawlessness, mistakes of the leadership, the government's neglect of its people, the inability to assume responsibility for one's own destiny?"

Irina answered. "Everything the government is now doing pushes us toward poverty." She wanted to say more, but her mother interrupted her once again, and Irina respectfully listened. "I have already lived my life, but I am worried about my granddaughters. Woman is a beast of burden and has no rights today." When she said this, I glanced at Irina's taut, gaunt face and saw the deep shadows under her eyes and her red-dyed hair whose white roots were showing. She looked a very old forty-four.

"We are constantly hearing about new laws and the protection of our rights, but these are only words. Every politician has a lot to say, but does nothing," her mother said. With tears once again flowing down her cheeks, she said, while sobbing, "We have had so many hopes and disappointments during the last seven decades. I want to do something for my granddaughter Nadya, but I am too old. The people who could have helped her are dead."

At that moment, Nadya stopped doing her homework and came over with a handkerchief. She wiped away her grandmother's tears and put her arm around her. "Nadya is diligent and hardworking, and I demand a great deal from her," Irina said. "She will speak three languages in a year and will also graduate from evening music school. It costs 40 rubles a month, but she can work and pay for a part of it."

"What do you want to be?" I asked Nadya. "An English interpreter," she said. Just for fun I switched from Russian to English and was amazed at her good command of English. If she focused on her English studies for the next few years, I told her, she might have an opportunity to study abroad. I knew of Russians who had received scholarships to study at colleges and universities in the United States; these awards were based on scholastic achievement rather than on money or influence.

I advised Nadya that she should improve her English and prepare for the college admittance exam for foreigners. If she passed, I would be willing to help her find a place at an American university. For the first time I saw her grandmother's face brighten, and Irina said quietly, "That will be our hope for the future."

5

BABUSHKA
NATASHA

*M*OSCOW USED TO BE a restful is-
land for my soul—a place where I could refuel with new energy. My
friends spoiled me with their love and attention. Their problems became
mine, and we solved them together. I was moved to hear "When you
come the sun begins to shine" or to receive a New Year's card with the
message, "If you disappear, Lois, my life will be dark, awful, and without
miracles." It was gratifying to be needed.

Perestroika had opened the emigration door for many old friends
whom I had met at the end of the 1970s when I lived in Moscow. At first I
tried to discourage them from leaving. "Perestroika will give you the opportunity to fulfill your dreams," I said. They answered, "It will take at
least two generations before reforms will be felt." I continued my argu-
ments, "In a new country it will be difficult to find a good job and close
friends like the ones you are leaving behind." The response was always
the same. "I must think about my children's future." Many of my friends
left the country between 1987 and 1992, and I miss them when I come to
Moscow.

Moscow had also become depressing for another reason. From summer 1990 until the following summer, every visit was accompanied by
bad news and insolvable problems. In the cozy surroundings of my one-
room flat my friends were used to receiving an infusion of hope and energy. Suddenly I felt as helpless as they.

In the early 1980s everyone worried about the threat of a third world
war. Ten years later they feared civil war, hunger, pogroms, and crime.
When I arrived at the airport during the winter of 1991, Masha, the adventurer, reprimanded me for bringing a fur coat. "That might cost your
life," she said. She had recently been beaten up by two prostitutes, whom
the police released without making any charges. The prostitutes were an-

gry that Masha had not permitted them to join the delegation of foreigners she was dining with in a restaurant. Anatoly told me about the murder of two men in front of his house. Natasha's dacha was vandalized. A Russian driver was beaten up in a parking lot and then stripped of his fashionable Western clothing. A taxi driver threatened to throw a German cameraman out of his cab on a dark rainy night if he did not pay in dollars. If my friends dared to walk on the streets at night, they usually carried some kind of protection, such as tear gas or a whistle. The private ownership of guns is strictly controlled, but this does not discourage people from purchasing weapons on the black market.

When Larissa returned to Moscow from a trip abroad she saw a banner in front of a school. It read, "Jews, leave the country." The wife of a German diplomat, who spoke German in the subway, was told by a drunken passenger, "You don't belong here."

A walk through my neighborhood was no more encouraging than the news I heard. Litter filled the streets and courtyards; the shelves of shops looked as though they had not been dusted for months; and shop windows wore such a grimy veil that I had to press my nose against them to see what was inside.

People in public places were even ruder and more aggressive than before. The woman who monitored the queue in a milk shop and decided how many people could enter at one time shouted at an intelligent but timid-looking customer, "You idiot, you are a real idiot." She repeated this insult three more times, and I was the only person who winced. Such language and vulgarity often flowed from the mouths of low-ranking civil servants who wanted to demonstrate their authority, and the downtrodden accepted this as normal behavior. The one time I saw a customer defend herself, the cashier, who was confident that no one would dare enter a complaint in the complaint book hanging on the wall behind her, refused to serve her.

Many shops were closed, and those that were open had very few items for sale. That situation persisted until April 1991, when prices rose astronomically. The shelves then filled with goods that the average citizen could not afford. The streets and shops of Moscow were no longer crowded with the 2 million tourists from elsewhere in the Soviet Union who came to the capital on shopping sprees. Signs in shops said tourists were no longer welcome; only people with Moscow identity cards could shop there. Long lines once meant that a foreign product was for sale. Now people lined up to buy staples. The scarcity of products and the new rationing system lightened the load of the babushkas, who were, and still are, the packhorses in Soviet families.

Capitalism has been legal since 1992; before that capitalists, called speculators or black marketeers, sold their goods privately so that they would not be arrested. Now they stood boldly on the streets selling whatever the market demanded. The sidewalk in front of the children's clothing and toy shop across from my apartment looked like a flea market every day. Mothers displayed baby shoes on top of carriages in which they lulled their babies to sleep. Fathers held on to their children with one hand and talked customers into buying toys they held in the other. Sometimes the items were for sale in the shop, but often customers preferred to pay several times the official price rather than stand in line for at least four hours. Other people came to barter items. I saw one woman exchange shoes for a skirt.

The majority of customers in Beriozka shops were locals who, in spite of the law, were no longer afraid to spend their dollars publicly. Soviets who owned Mercedes, the most prestigious foreign car in the country, were proud to display their treasure, even if it had been bought with illegally earned money.

Only the rich could afford the outrageous prices at the private market. When eggs and meat were not available in state stores, they could be bought at the private market: One egg cost 3 rubles and meat 25 rubles a kilo. Inflation forced many people, like my taxi driver who had studied to be an engineer, to leave their professions for better-paying jobs. After one year of earning only 140 rubles a month as an engineer, he became a taxi driver. "I have two children who are four and ten years old. On my former salary," he said, "I couldn't afford to buy them pants for 60 rubles." His official salary as a cab driver was now 200 rubles, supplemented by the 800 rubles earned on the side by driving the cab at night.

The life-style of the nouveau riche was as dramatic as the poverty. Old people sat, with hands outstretched, on the streets and in pedestrian underpasses. They crossed themselves in gratitude for every coin dropped in front of them. In summer the homeless camped on the green square in front of the Kiev railroad station, and their barefoot, unwashed children clung to passersby until they either gave them money or managed to tear themselves loose. The homeless were members of racial minorities who had fled republics that waged pogroms against them. Twelve thousand victims who had lost their homes, belongings, and jobs came to Moscow to demand compensation from the central government. The government refuses to recognize their status as "refugees" with legal rights.

A woman, clothed in tatters, cuddled a sleeping baby on her lap. She sat on the steps of a shop in my neighborhood and her grief-stricken expression moved me to stop and talk to her. She came from Moldavia where her home and belongings had been destroyed during an earthquake. She had come to Moscow to receive remuneration for her losses. Her temporary home was a railroad station. An older passerby, overhearing our conversation, said in a distraught voice, "It's a shame that the government does not take care of such people." I asked the woman what she needed and returned a few minutes later with food and clothing.

Some street scenes reinforced my feeling that I was living in a world of crazy contradictions. Buses carried advertisements for Sanyo video recorders, and Communist slogans on buildings were replaced by ads for products from Western firms. For whom were these ads intended? Such items could only be bought with foreign currency. At a time when mothers were worrying about where they could find food for their children, a large poster advertised the coming international People and Food Fair.

Some vodka shop customers brought their own bottles; two bottles entitled them to buy a half liter—no limit. A bottle shortage was blamed on cooperative owners who had sold bottles as crushed glass to the West for foreign currency. Then coupons allowing every Muscovite one bottle a month were issued. This did not stop alcoholics and other resourceful people from buying vodka. They simply bought vodka coupons from non-drinkers.

Customers in stores complained about the rationing system and talked at home about the energy crisis. My apartment was unbearably over-heated until the winter of 1991, and then it was so cold that I had to wear so many layers of clothing that I looked like a cabbage. One day the tem-perature outside dropped to 30 below and my radiator quit completely. I had only cold water, but not for long. While foreigners receive almost im-mediate service, Russians do not. My neighbors, who lived in an old, run-down building, were told they would have to wait weeks before their hot water and heat could be restored. They were no better off than my Ar-menian friends, living in Yerevan, who had become accustomed to cold radiators and only a few hours of electricity and water daily. Their prob-lems, however, were the result of an energy crisis caused by a long-time feud with neighboring Azerbaijan. Azerbaijan restricts the flow of oil to Armenia.

Deteriorating living conditions and increasing daily hardships partic-ularly affected pensioners, invalids, and mothers with young children, while, at the same time, young people who were willing to work hard lived well. Their motto was individualism, not collectivism. Cooperative businesses gave them the chance to earn a lot of money, but this was not the only attraction. The twenty-year-old son of a friend said, "I never wanted to be a slave to the government that exploited my parents their whole lives. I want to have responsibility and be free."

"Do the masses really want freedom?" I asked my intellectual friends during the wee hours of a long night. One said, "They don't need democ-racy or perestroika. They want a stable life with guarantees. Give them sausage and they will be willing to live in a cage." Another said, "Freedom has no value here, especially to the poor, who are in the majority. Free-dom does not give them a better life. Being a free man is an abstract idea. Since the first czar everything has been decided by someone else. A per-son does not even have the right to choose where he lives or works."

A journalist recalled an article written by a colleague about visiting a Dutch prison. The text ended with the phrase, "I dream of being a pris-oner in a Dutch prison." "Dutch prisoners live like the *nomenklatura,* who are on vacation somewhere in a privileged rest home," my friend said ironically. "The criminal in the West is isolated from society for his crime, but he is respected and treated like a human being. Here no one is treated like a human being," he said.

My former cleaning woman was one of the few people I knew who was neither cynical nor embittered about life. "I am already a pensioner and have lived my life, but I have hope for my grandchild," Natasha said. She was confident that future generations would grow up in a world knowing their rights and able to defend them.

I was the first foreigner Natasha had ever met when she came to work for me in the late 1970s. I did not speak Russian at that time, and she did not know a foreign language, but we understood each other "with hands and feet," she used to say. She was an angelic soul, who had an aura of calm and cheer. After she overcame her initial fears and shyness, she treated me as though I were her daughter. In her opinion I was too thin and she tried to fatten me up with homemade *pelmeni* (ravioli) and cream puffs. I usually slept five hours a night and she considered this three hours too few. Occasionally I gave in to her entreaties and took a nap in the afternoon.

Before she met me, she had the impression that all foreigners were rich, spoiled, and enjoyed a life of luxury. Twelve years later she revealed that she had a rude awakening on her first day of work. "When I arrived at 9 A.M. the kitchen was already clean, the washing machine was running, and the apartment was in order. You had curlers in your hair and sat typing. In a short time I understood that a rich person rises at 5 A.M. and begins to work in order to afford a comfortable life-style," she said.

I did not lose touch with Natasha when I left Moscow in 1981. Several times a year I returned to work on subjects for books and to see my friends. At the end of the 1980s I received an accreditation as a journalist, which had two advantages: I no longer had to apply for a visa for every visit; and I had a flat of my own for future visits. Natasha volunteered to look after it, which gave us the opportunity to see each other even more often.

On one occasion Natasha complained about a rapidly growing mouse family that had found shelter in my flat, and I replied, "Leave them in peace." After they consumed several kilos of imported Swiss chocolate bars and added my clothing and books to their menu, Natasha declared war. She wanted to use mouse poison or mousetraps to eliminate them, but I favored more humane treatment. I brought a "live mousetrap" from Germany, which proved to be effective but bothersome. I was awakened several times every night as one after another was trapped. After each "catch" I drowsily stumbled down three flights of stairs to the street, where I looked for a patch of grass that was free of a preying cat. But still my mouse population did not seem to decrease. Natasha then decided to spread cat hair around the flat. Fortunately, this smell made the mice change their address, and I once again enjoyed living alone.

Natasha has hardly changed physically since I met her. She could still wear the dresses I had given her, although size 22 was now a little snug. Only her glasses were a little thicker. Unlike most Soviet women, whose hard life rapidly aged them, Natasha remained remarkably young looking and active for her seventy-four years. When I asked her what her secret was, she laughed in a charming, girlish way, and said, "I have been working since I was seventeen, and work has kept me young."

We had grown closer to each other over the years, and I was happy when she stopped addressing me as "Madame Lois" and called me just plain Lois. I spoke to her as I would to a good friend and this behavior amazed her. "I am a simple, ordinary person, from a working-class background. You have a higher education and speak many languages. You talk to me as though I am your equal, if not one step higher."

"All our lives we have heard that there are no class differences in our society. Communism also teaches that everyone is equal. The reality is different. For the working class equality means that everyone should live on the same level. Those, like cooperative owners, who try to improve their living standard through hard work, are hated and envied. The working class even tries to sabotage their success," she said.

Natasha admired people who worked hard and often complained about the number of "good for nothings" who were not willing to work, but, at the same time, dreamed of a life of luxury. She was sympathetic to emigrants who had left the Soviet Union. "They received no recognition for their achievements and talent here." With her usual optimism she said, "I hope they will eventually return with their new knowledge and experience and help their motherland. We desperately need foreign managers and specialists who can teach us how to work properly and organize our economy."

She remembered a time when Russia exported butter to European countries and was rich. "It will be rich again," she said, and then quoted the Russian proverb, "We need only one Russian village to build a great Russia."

Natasha's flushed face and raised voice told me that she had something important to say, and I did not interrupt her for the next few minutes. "My family has always worked hard. I began standing in lines when I was seven years old. My son had three jobs at one time. It's a pity that my granddaughter and her generation are different. They are used to relaxing and being waited on. They are spoiled and unable to cope with life. It would be unfair to blame this entirely on the system in which both parents work and the children receive their education on the streets. The parents are also guilty. Our life was hard and we wanted our children to have a better life. When I grew up the shoemaker taught his son to be a shoemaker. My father was a bookkeeper, so I learned bookkeeping. Today no one wants to follow in the footsteps of his father, unless he is a privileged person."

"It is difficult to convince young people today to work and live honestly. Ethics, morals, and politics do not influence their lives. If they believe in anything it is the power of money."

Natasha proudly recalled how modestly she and her husband had lived while saving for their first car. Since then they had also purchased a color television, a VCR, and a washing machine. Unlike many other families, who earned money legally or illegally on the side, they lived only on their official salaries.

Behind Natasha's soft voice and carefree laugh was a powerhouse who benevolently ruled the family. She had brought up her granddaughter, Marcia, and had taken care of her own household at the same time. She was also in charge of the budget and made all the important decisions for her family and her son's family. One of the major events of the past few years had been joining the two households in order that each family had more living space. Natasha managed this complicated exchange, which gained them a comfortable five-room apartment. At the same time it caused much more work for her because now she had to cook, shop, and clean for five people.

Natasha's friends knew that she was the pillar of her family and be-seeched her to take care of herself. Her son and granddaughter depended on her, and her eighty-six-year-old husband had started ailing and re-quired more care.

I had met her husband on several occasions and found him charming and dynamic. Natasha was proud of him and boasted about the many ac-colades he received when he worked as a cameraman for films. After twenty-five years on the job he was offered privileges that made Natasha's life a little easier. Every week he could order scarce products, such as cream, yogurt, fish, or sausage. The family had to pay only 50 percent of the cost for rent, gas, and electricity. But such benefits did not impress Marcia, who said to her grandmother one day, "We have nothing com-pared to my friends." Natasha's answer was, "They may have more money and possessions, but we enjoy privileges earned through hard, honest work."

While Natasha ruled the roost at home, she came to me from time to time to share her problems. She called me her "tranquilizer." One after-noon she burst into tears, saying my apartment was the only place where she could cry. Her husband had inoperable cancer and there was no medicine available to reduce his severe pain. Only the night before she had seen on television how the head of a drugstore had hidden car-tons of medicine in a cellar so that she could profit personally from the sales. Even in hospitals nurses withheld medication and doctors stopped writing prescriptions because of the catastrophic shortage of medicine. At the same time it was public knowledge that leading gov-ernment functionaries and their families were treated in special clinics and hospitals equipped with the latest Western technology and medi-cine.

Natasha apologized for burdening me with her problems, but she could not speak to anyone else. Within a few days medicine ordered from Germany arrived, which gave her husband temporary relief. Over the next few weeks his condition deteriorated, and she remained at his side day and night. On my return to Moscow, I heard that he had died the week before in the hospital.

Being a practical person, Natasha had prepared for her husband's death by stocking up on food for the traditional dinners that would follow his death. Her hours of standing in lines paid off. When the tragic day came her two freezers were full of tongue, chicken, and other delicacies. The state also assisted by giving her a stamped copy of the death certificate, which entitled her to buy 3 kilos [13 pounds] of smoked sausage, a can of caviar, a can of Chinese stew, and, most important, 20 bottles of vodka for the customary banquet on the ninth and fortieth days after the death. The first sumptuous feast took place right after the funeral, when thirty guests returned to the family flat to consume the meal relatives had prepared.

Her husband's death ended his unbearable pain, and Natasha promised to go to the countryside to rest and renew her strength, which she would need in the coming months. While her husband was ill, her forty-eight-year-old son was, like his father, diagnosed with inoperable cancer. This tragic news had forced her to make another tough decision while her husband was alive. The family plot in a cemetery had space for only one more person, and she decided to leave it for her son. Since cemeteries are overcrowded and obtaining a new burial place is impossible without money and connections, Natasha chose to have her husband cremated.

"Life is sometimes so unjust," I said, thinking about her son's terminal illness. Regaining her composure, Natasha said, "Laws can be just as unjust." Changing the subject gave her strength, and she could vent her anger against something practical. "Have you heard about the funeral reform?" she asked. "That was the most thoughtless and personal blow against honest people, particularly the pensioners. If anyone still had faith in the government, this new law destroyed his last belief," she said.

The announcement of this shocking reform was made in January 1991, during the nightly national news program. Soviet citizens were told that they had three days to change their 50- and 100-ruble bills for smaller denominations. After three days these bills would be invalid. The official explanation for this reform was that it was intended to fight the shadow economy—black marketeers and the Mafia—and those who possessed millions of illegal rubles abroad.

The designers of this reform were so convinced of its rightness that they did not consider the catastrophic results that could follow. Panic broke out. The country was paralyzed for three days. No one went to work. The law stated that each working person was permitted to exchange only one month's salary and pensioners, 200 rubles. Those who wanted to exchange more than this amount had to give a written explanation to a commission, and each case would be reviewed.

Traditionally Russians saved their entire lives for their funeral, and old people usually kept this money at home because they did not trust banks nor did they want to burden their family with excessive funeral expenses resulting from high bribes. The grandmother of a friend told me that she had 5,000 rubles under her mattress. She did not put it in the bank because she wanted her family to be able to have access to it as soon as she died. Otherwise they would have had to wait as long as six months for bank formalities to be settled. This old woman was better off than others who had no families. Her children would find a way to exchange her large savings. If she were alone she might have had to forfeit a considerable amount of her savings.

When pensioners who had no family heard about this reform, they went to the banks that night and stood in line all night so they would be there when the banks opened. Some died of heart attacks and others were admitted to hospitals. In Moscow the shrill sound of ambulance sirens kept the capital awake on this night of doom.

The following morning, old people experienced another shock. The banks had not been informed about this decree and therefore were not prepared to exchange money. They could only give citizens a piece of paper that guaranteed their money would be returned to them. But who could believe in a piece of paper?

Shrewd people, who spent their lives outwitting the system, found methods to avoid lines and explanations about the source of their wealth. Some went to airports or railroad stations and bought a handful of tickets with 50- and 100-ruble bills. They would return the tickets later and receive a refund. At the private market the main business the next day was exchanging big bills for small ones at high rates.

In factories, educational and research institutes, and government offices, the exchange of large bills for small went smoothly. Officials and employees received receipts that guaranteed they would receive new bills in the next few days. The days stretched to weeks, but in the end everyone was satisfied.

During the next weeks money problems arose in stores, post offices, and banks. Rumors spread that 25-ruble bills would be invalid soon, and customers and store employees refused to accept them. A friend of mine, who was in line in a bank, heard the announcement, "People who are not willing to accept 25-ruble bills should leave."

Another part of this ill-considered reform was to forbid people from withdrawing more than 500 rubles a month from their savings accounts. In order to prevent this, customers received a stamp in their domestic passport when a withdrawal was made. This was one of the first times the system outwitted those who usually found a way around a regulation or law.

"The banking rule is unfair," Natasha said. "That is my money that I earned honestly. I should have the right to withdraw any amount from my bank account when I need it." I agreed with her and said, "The government is expropriating its own people." Meanwhile signs that proclaimed how safe, comfortable, and advantageous it was to put money in savings banks discreetly disappeared.

The new banking system created all kinds of problems. "If I want to buy something expensive, I must go to the bank, which will issue a check only for the official price of the item," Natasha said. "But everyone knows that the real price is three times more. By the time this transaction is completed, the article that I wanted to buy will most likely have disappeared." "Why didn't people demonstrate against this unjust law?" I asked. "When did they have time?" Natasha asked. "They had to stand in lines for days."

Although this reform was allegedly directed against the Mafia, it hardly penalized its members. Through their connections they had heard about it in advance and had invested their hundreds of thousands of rubles in property, antiques, and foreign currency. Other insiders, like Natasha's neighbor, who was the wife of a general, changed their money before the official announcement was made. "Now I understand why my son's last bimonthly salary was paid in 50- and 100-ruble notes. The banks had already been emptied of small bills by those who knew about the reform in advance," Natasha said.

Natasha was certain that the money reform, which acquired the epithet Funeral Reform, was not intentionally directed against pensioners. "The problem of the leadership is that it acts without considering the possible consequences. When a person acquires power, it corrupts him, and he loses touch with reality. He is mainly interested in a comfortable life with a dacha, a bank account in the West, and influential friends who can provide for him and his family. He will never have to worry about paying for his funeral, and so it does not occur to him that this could be a problem for others. In Russia there is a proverb that describes the mentality of the government leaders. 'The well-fed is not a friend of the hungry.'"

Like the majority of Muscovites, Natasha had been a supporter of Gorbachev; but now we both considered him a tragic figure. "He created a revolution in the world and tried the same in his own country, but he did not succeed. No one can create order in this chaotic country. It would be a mistake to replace him because we don't know what tomorrow will bring. Those who hold power have used it for their own well-being, and he is no exception. We crave the truth and want to trust someone, but there is no such person. We believed the Minister of Economics when he denied rumors that a money reform would take place. Only after announcing it did he admit that the government had been working on this reform for one year. Our only hope for the future is to produce a decent, honest leader who will be an example for the country. This leader must understand that a reform like the Funeral Reform gives the masses reason to distrust and despise the government. If trust and credibility are lacking, the people have no reason to work for a better future."

6

THE SOLDIERS
ARE NOT HOMESICK

*D*URING MY YEARS in the Soviet Union the life of the military remained a mystery to me. For security reasons members of the army, navy, and air force live in isolation and are not permitted to have personal contact with foreigners. I had spoken with the sons of friends who had served their hard, two-year obligation in the army, but I had never met officers and their families.

After the reunification of Germany, an unprecedented situation occurred. The Soviet army, reputedly one of the most modern in the world, suddenly found itself in NATO territory. This meant that Soviet soldiers stationed in what had been East Germany could no longer be isolated from the Western world and that Soviet army garrisons in Germany were opened to visitors with special permission.

In July 1991 I was permitted to visit a Soviet military enclave called Wuensdorf, about an hour's drive from Berlin. The photographer who accompanied me and I had difficulty finding this town because only one road sign, about 49 kilometers from our destination, indicated that such a place exists. There were no more road signs after we were pointed in the right direction. Local residents helped us, but in spite of their directions we did not find the main visitor's entrance to Wuensdorf immediately and ended up driving around the enormous fenced-in army post. Signs in Russian and German indicated that the area behind the walls and barbed wire was restricted. Later I heard that the 2,700 German residents living in Wuensdorf had not had access to the garrison since 1953. Only high East German government functionaries had special passes, allegedly for business purposes.

We drove from one closed gate to the next at the advice of the soldiers guarding the garrison. We even went to the "Russian railroad" station—directly across from the German railroad station—where Russians were lined up to buy tickets for the regular Moscow Express. When we finally arrived at the main gate we were told that the press officer, Colonel Leonid Loss, had just left after waiting for us more than an hour. It would take a few minutes to locate him and during that time a polite, blond soldier, who looked as though he had just begun to shave, unlocked the door to a room that was attached to his guard station. He invited us to make ourselves comfortable at a square table with hard wooden chairs. This was most likely the reception room for foreign guests waiting for escorts to pick them up.

I was too curious to sit still more than a moment and joined the young soldier guarding the gate. Each person entering or leaving the garrison had to show him an identity card or written permission before he would open or close the gate by hand.

The youthful-looking Colonel Loss, who wore a mustache—I guessed to make him appear older—eventually arrived. He motioned to the guard to open the gate for us and led the way in his Russian Volga. The main road had a fresh coat of tar and newly painted white lines. As we followed his driver down a breathtaking alley between towering trees and undulating green fields, I forgot for a moment where I was. This idyllic and peaceful setting was a far cry from our drive through polluted and noisy East Berlin that morning. There, the gutted shells of Trabbies (East German cars) rusted in streets lined by buildings with pockmarked and peeling facades.

Young soldiers cutting the high grass with sickles and gathering the hay reminded me I was in a military garrison, not on an island. The beautiful wooded area was followed by ugly gray and sand-colored barrack-like buildings built for German air force and army officers. The only touch of color was a fire hydrant being painted red by a soldier. The high voices of nursery school children walking hand in hand, accompanied by their teacher, and the sound of a baby crying did not fit the rigid military surroundings.

A towering statue of Lenin stood in front of the massive cultural hall where we were to meet the wives of officers with whom I was to spend the day. The first woman to greet me was Svetlana, an attractive and self-confident Russian, who at once left an impression of competence. There are thousands of Svetlana-types in the Soviet Union who are the power behind their bosses. Without them things would be more chaotic than they already are in the country.

Svetlana was chair of the women's committee, whose main function is to plan cultural programs and extracurricular activities for officers and their families. She came from Lvov in Ukraine, where she had been a French teacher. Four years earlier her husband was assigned to work as an engineer for the armed forces in Germany, and she joined him there.

She had helped organize my program and introduced me to the blond and boyish-looking Igor, a twenty-three-year-old lieutenant who had studied German for five years at the armed forces foreign language institute in Moscow. He would be my interpreter, if I needed one. I then met Olga, who was temperamentally and physically Svetlana's opposite. She was soft, feminine, and retiring. Her dark green shirtwaist dress matched her bespectacled green eyes, and she had blond hair and pale flawless skin. Olga worked as a gynecologist in the garrison's clinic, and her husband conducted the seventy-man orchestra attached to the military staff's headquarters.

She had met her husband when she was visiting her parents in the Caucasus more than twenty years earlier, she said. At that time she was a medical student, and he was studying at a music institute in Moscow. After completing his studies he was chosen to attend the military music college and began a career as a musician in the army. Now he is a colonel and entitled to retire at this rank in six years at the age of fifty.

Her husband's military career took them to different cities in the Soviet Union where she worked as a doctor. Their first foreign post had been Prague, where they and their two sons lived for five years; Wuensdorf was their second foreign post.

Their twenty-one-year-old son was studying law in Riga, which Olga regarded as home. They had lived there more than six years, and more importantly, they had an apartment there. Knowing how indulged and overprotected Soviet children are, I asked Olga if she worried about her son living alone. "Today's youth are much less afraid than we were. They are also more self-confident." To prove her point she said, "Our son chose to study law because he wants to change something during his life. His aim is to fight against injustice."

I knew that Latvian had recently become the newly independent country's administrative language and asked how her Russian son, whose first language was Russian, was managing. "He is now studying Latvian," she said, "and he has to pass a language exam before he receives his diploma." She admitted that she probably would have to learn the language when she returned. She recalled attending a meeting at her institute in Riga at which 70 percent of the participants spoke Russian, but the administration insisted that Latvian be spoken.

Her son had not yet served in the army, an obligation he faced upon graduation. As a Latvian resident, however, he had the right to choose between serving as a soldier or doing community work. His current preference was to use his professional skills in a civilian job at the customs office at Riga's port.

The Russian Republic had not yet enacted a law recognizing the rights of conscientious objectors, and I asked my hosts what they thought about such a status. As usual the outspoken, politically active Svetlana was the first to speak, while Olga remained silent. She maintained that the only acceptable grounds for a conscientious objector were religion and health. "Fifty percent of the soldiers are Muslims from Central Asia," she said. "Often problems arise when they refuse to perform jobs they are assigned in the army. For example, the Koran forbids a man to do 'woman's work,' and many consider washing toilets and floors a violation of the Koran."

"What about people who object to military service because of their conscience?" I asked. "The army is necessary because it makes a man out of a soldier," she said. She realized that this answer was not very convincing and to back up her statement, she cited a program she had seen on Soviet television, the only channel the Soviet armed forces receive in Germany. At that time its reporting was the least objective of any channel, as far as I knew. My Russian friends stopped watching this nationwide channel, which they nicknamed The Voice of Gorbachev, in the fall of 1990 and returned to their pre-glasnost habit of listening to foreign broadcasts such as Deutsche Welle and the BBC.

Young men were interviewed during the program, Svetlana said, and "almost all replied that every man should serve in the army and defend his motherland." I then introduced the controversial subject of deserters. This problem had become particularly acute after German reunification, when an estimated two hundred soldiers and officers sought political asylum in Germany.

The *Moscow News,* and *Ogonok* had covered this subject, and I asked Olga and Svetlana if they read these publications. They read not only these, they said, but also *Pravda, Izvestia,* and others. This gave me the opportunity to ask their opinions about two controversial articles I had read.

The June 1991 *Moscow News* had published an article about a thirty-year-old first lieutenant, Anatoly, who was assigned to East Germany in 1986 and deserted in summer 1990. After serving two years in Afghanistan, he said, "I have already killed. But there God forgave me. That was a foreign country, an unknown people. And I also had the feeling that it had something to do with enemies. But who are we fighting against in the Caucasus? And the command will come to shoot; it always comes. I complained to my commander. He began to threaten me: 'We will bring you to trial and throw you in prison.' And I realized, this is it, you have to disappear."

After Afghanistan, he said, military service in East Germany was "no mere prison—it was a concentration camp. Every day officers tried to destroy me, not just physically, but morally. ... East Germany was a special zone; there they had their own rules. For example, they purposely punished the superior for our mistakes so that he would unleash his anger on us. The main point is that everyone lives in a state of constant fear. You hear over and over again, 'You are the lowest form of filth.' Officers try to humiliate you and break your will. ... Once a man is broken he doesn't talk anymore. He believes that he is guilty. He holds his tongue and cowers. Another form of conditioning ... is the 'lock-in.' The commanding officer can decide, for example, when money is stolen from a soldier that all officers remain in the barracks instead of going home to their families. This means that everyone is guilty and must be punished.

"The young men who are sent to East Germany are really good guys to begin with. Here they make criminals out of them. I am making this judgment based on those under my command and those with whom I have spoken. A man who is locked in a cage—often there is no leave for an entire year—becomes an animal. When he does not receive even the least amount of care, it makes no difference to him whether he steals or kills someone. Hunger clouds the brain. It may seem bizarre, but the soldiers here don't have the slightest fear of being arrested. Punishment gives the recruits a chance to rest.

"Much worse than arrest for the soldiers is the delayed demobilization, when the commander does not release them for several months. Then the commander can do whatever he wants with them. The soldiers give everything to him, even their miserable DM 25 pay. There is another form of punishment. Before releasing a group of soldiers for leave, they are ordered to the commander's office. They are separated from each other, and everything they were planning to take home with them is confiscated. They are frisked and robbed right down to the smallest trinket that a son might want to give his mother as a present."

Anatoly was living in an undisclosed location because he said, "The KGB has the longest arms in the world." He was afraid they would kidnap him, something they had allegedly tried to do to other deserters. He hoped the German government would grant him asylum, but the Soviet government was putting pressure on Germany to turn over deserters. Until then, the German response had been, "Whoever seeks political asylum here shall enjoy the complete protection of the law. Until that person's future is duly determined, and if necessary decided by the courts, he shall have the right to remain in our country."

The letter of a conscripted soldier, published in *Ogonyok* (Number 6, 1991), was clearer and more detailed than the first lieutenant's account in the *Moscow News.* He wrote: "I deserted from the Soviet Army not only because during the first ten months the 'older ones' persisted in beating me, a newcomer, but also because I suddenly realized that this service was of no use to me or to my homeland. Military service can embitter one to the point of saying, 'I can't take it anymore.'

"My name is Sergei. My military service began in November 1989. I served with the infantry in East Germany. During the first three days the 'old ones,' or the 'skulls,' made it clear to me how one could best survive: 'according to military regulations' or 'not according to military regulations.' To survive 'according to military regulations' meant working for them for two years. At least they would not beat you, that was true, but you lived in such an atmosphere that the only thing left was to hang yourself. You had to perform the most menial tasks and were forced to steal packages, laundry, and soap. To live 'not according to military regulations' meant serving the 'old ones' and the others for nine months until you became a veteran, and then you could put the new ones to work for you.

"What would you, a newcomer, be beaten for? For everything. The word 'no' did not exist. If you had to go to the end of the world to get something, that was your problem. Go and fetch cigarettes, matches, needles and thread, white material to tack under worn collars (for that we stole bed sheets), and so on.

"We had to perform all kinds of chores for the 'old ones,' such as cleaning the toilets and the hallways, and washing the 'old ones'' underwear. At night they even asked us to find potatoes and somehow cook them. I make no secret of the fact that I stole from German gardens and vegetable patches. Once I stole a ham and some conserves from someone's cellar. If I failed to carry out my assignments, I would be beaten on the chest or face. My chest was always blue. Not one of the senior officers ever asked why. They would use a stool to beat my kidneys—that was called 'drinking a little beer.' Of the DM 28 I received, I had to give 20 to the 'old ones.' We were always hungry, and all we had to eat was boiled porridge, sometimes with a little bacon. Many of us suffered from diarrhea, vomiting, and stomach pains. We were allowed to wash ourselves only once a week, despite the fact that we had to run 8 kilometers every day in uniform. During the last two months I scratched myself until I bled. The doctor in Berlin diagnosed this as scabies.

"The officers saw everything but acted as though it was normal. During the last four months we slept in tents in temperatures below 2 or 3

degrees [centigrade] because the barracks had to be repaired. The surrounding woods were filthy. On Sunday the excrement was buried and
on Monday we would empty our bowels again in the woods.

"I never read anything in the Soviet press about the number of soldiers
who committed suicide or how many died during peacetime.

"In any case, soldiers were always guarded carefully, as carefully as
prisoners. German television reported that 150 soldiers deserted to Germany in one week. Fifty-seven of them requested political asylum. The
others hid in the forest.

"There are many changes occurring now in my life. Will there be
changes as well for the Soviet Army? And who is responsible for the
army? As always—no one?"

Svetlana had read this letter and said, "I know army life and admit that
some of what he wrote is true, but not everything. He has exaggerated the
situation." Igor, the young officer, did not agree. "I believe what he said. I
never wanted to be a simple soldier and know that under certain circumstances the life of a soldier can be a nightmare."

"Why is the life of a soldier so inhumane and difficult?" I asked. Igor
responded, "This is a problem of society. Before a soldier is drafted he is
brought up in the same environment as his superiors. Problems come to
a head in the army. This is why everything the soldier wrote could be
true."

"Deserters are unpopular in every army," he continued. Svetlana
added, "They have betrayed their country and deserve to be punished."
She smugly talked about a film "we have made" about the deserters who
had returned. "They came back voluntarily because they did not find
what they were seeking. Now they regret their behavior. They know that
they have damaged the reputation of the army."

I asked about their punishment, and she said, "Some will be severely
criticized at a special meeting. Others will be arrested based on their
crime. The severity of the punishment is determined by the behavior and
conscience of the accused."

Igor did not agree completely with Svetlana. He said, "Each case
should be judged on its merits. Some soldiers might have been forced to

make this decision." I was too diplomatic to ask about the more than 30,000 soldiers rumored to have committed suicide in the Soviet armed forces over the last years.

I mentioned that the image of the army had been tainted since it was involved in bloodbaths in the Caucasus and the Baltic republics. Svetlana interrupted to say, "The people have always loved the army. The media are guilty for this hostility. This is an artificial problem." Her opinion did not differ from that of arch-conservative Major General Igor Podgorny, one of the deputy chiefs of staff of the West Group of the Soviet Armed Forces stationed in Germany. In May 1991 he spoke at a Friedrich Ebert Foundation meeting in Bonn and accused the Soviet media of printing lies about the army. Unlike Svetlana and Olga, he said he refused to read publications such as *Moscow News* and *Ogonyok.*

"What should the role of the army be?" I asked. Everyone agreed in principle that the army should not have a police function. Svetlana justi-fied the army's "uncustomary role" in national conflicts with the remark, "The situation has become so complicated that the only stabilizing force is the army."

"The image of the army can be improved when it institutes reforms," I said. Igor implied that the soldiers, young officers, and senior officers were not always in agreement about the role of the army. In his opinion the army should be smaller so that more money could be used for civilian purposes. He also hoped that the army would work with NATO to help maintain peace.

Svetlana cited an army reform that she considered significant. "The party no longer plays the leading role. The women's organization has the same authority and right to make decisions as the party committee," she said proudly. The reticent Olga, who had not spoken about politics until now, said, "The Communist party should no longer play a leading role in the country. We should have more political parties." This was a bold re-mark, I thought, for a long-standing party member, but it was well known that officers had to belong to the party.

It was clear to me that my conversation partners were selected as exem-plary representatives of the armed forces, and they were not as free to express their personal opinions as, for example, former Major General Vladimir Dudnik. In an article about the Soviet Army in *Die Zeit,* on May 24, 1991, Dudnik dealt openly with the declining image of the army. He wrote about the conflict in Afghanistan where "the highest level of command, which really was to blame, was naturally not held responsible, and instead the blame was placed on the Soviet Army." Then he mentioned the events in Tbilisi, Baku, and the Baltic republics where the army "was forced to carry out orders that were against its nature. They became involved in internal ethnic and political conflicts. ... Now that the image of the foreign enemy has been destroyed, the monolith of our armed forces suddenly stands without a purpose. So we have found an internal enemy—the people."

He also wrote about strife in the army. "The officers mistrust the generals, and the generals in turn blame the officers for the same offenses. Military training is very poor. The warships are run down and defective. The aircraft are not secure. ..." The problems of the army were no different from those of society, and the officers have no faith in the future.

During a recent conference for the entire armed forces, Dudnik said that no reforms were discussed. "Instead, every form of metaphor was used to describe the 'Lenin-like patience' of the Soviet president in his 'attempt to reach national reconciliation.'"

Leaving behind controversial subjects, I switched to the banal and asked Olga about her typical day. Being a woman of few words, she talked about her day as though it was a railroad timetable. She rose at 6 A.M. to prepare her son for school and make breakfast for her husband. Her work in the hospital began at 8 A.M. and ended at 2 P.M.

She became a little more talkative when I prodded her to discuss how the deutsche mark had changed her life. Just as she began to speak, Colonel Loss said it was time to go to an orchestra rehearsal being conducted by Olga's husband. Joking, I chided him for interrupting the discussion at this particular moment and said I preferred to continue the conversation. Svetlana supported me, and together we overruled his suggestion.

Since July 1, 1990, members of the Soviet armed forces in Germany have been paid in deutsche marks, and the deutsche mark dominates their lives. It corrupted some, and made thieves out of others. Some of the older soldiers confiscated the meager earnings of the younger soldiers. German businessmen and Soviet emigrants bribed high-ranking military officers to sign contracts with their firms to supply the West Group of the Soviet Armed Forces with food and consumer goods. Many of these items were sold in garrison shops, which had a wider range of items than the foreign currency stores in Moscow.

Olga earned DM 700 a month, and her husband DM 1,200 during the summer of 1991. When she said this, I quickly calculated that this amounted to around 34,000 rubles on the black market in the Soviet Union, where the average monthly salary was under 300 rubles. Their first "important" purchase with their deutsche marks, Olga said, was a television set. Her friends were saving for a VCR, washing machine, video camera, and a secondhand car. When I asked what make of car they wanted to buy, the women said it must be cheap, and Igor added, "It is better to buy a Russian car that can be serviced in the Soviet Union."

Igor was single and said his living conditions were similar to those of many families in the Soviet Union. He shared a three-room communal flat with another single officer and a married officer with a child. Unlike many others, he saved his monthly salary of DM 800 for traveling.

Most Western articles sold in the garrison's stores were less expensive than items in Berlin shops because Wuensdorf had a special status. It was treated like a foreign country, and everything "imported" was duty free. Olga and Svetlana spent about DM 600 a month for foods such as fruits, vegetables, beverages, sausage, and cheese, which they bought in garrison and local stores, such as the Aldi chain. In addition they received a salary in rubles that they spent on staples, such as meat, butter, grain products, potatoes, cabbage, fish, sour cream, milk, and eggs, sent in from the Soviet Union. Like their countrymen, they were given ration cards that limited the amount they could buy.

After shopping and doing housework Olga helped her son with his homework. His summer holiday had just begun, and she suggested that we visit him at the Pioneer camp, a five-minute car ride away.

The fourteen-year-old Seryozha greeted us at the camp's entrance, and his mother behaved like a typical Soviet mother who is used to pampering her son until he becomes a pensioner. She adjusted his jogging jacket and jogging pants and combed his hair, which he patiently tolerated. Seryozha led the way and showed us the picturesque park-like surroundings located on a large lake. For twenty-six days 150 fortunate Soviet children between the ages of seven and fifteen could holiday here. The highlight was going to the discotheque each evening where the children danced and watched current Soviet films. On the day of my visit the boys were preparing for "The Girls Day," which would take place the following day, when "Miss Camper" would be chosen.

While walking past the athletic field I was distracted by a young boy with short hair and a long curl hanging down his back. For some reason I did not identify this modern Western hairstyle with the son of a Soviet military officer.

Seryozha did not speak German and was too shy to practice English with me, which was his foreign language in school. When I asked if he was homesick for Riga, he said, "I like living in Wuensdorf where we have normal living conditions." I asked him what "normal" meant, and he fell silent.

When we walked through one of the dorms Colonel Loss opened a door of a room in which six young boys were taking their afternoon nap and waved to his son. The camp holiday cost him only 37 rubles, he said, and I remarked that this was considerably less than he would have to spend on food for his son if he were at home. "He has even gained weight here," he said, and then talked about the day's menu, which included three large meals and two small snacks.

Colonel Loss regretted that the Soviet children no longer received invitations to holiday with German families. The summer before reunification two thousand children had been guests of East Germans, and after reunification not a single invitation was extended.

Reunification brought positive and negative changes. Colonel Loss, who sounded like a spokesman for the government, diplomatically said, "Reunification is a continuation of new thinking and new politics. All of the officers here support the new politics of our government, and we have witnessed the concrete results of our politics in Germany. Naturally it is up to the people to decide if they want to live divided or united."

"You know, there was speculation that the Soviet Union wanted to prevent this reunification process. I must tell you that we had no orders to undertake any measures on the borders. Shevardnadze said that a conservative force stood in the way of reunification, which was widely interpreted to mean the army. The former Russian ambassador in East Berlin corrected this impression with his statement that the Soviet army had received commands not to interfere." Once again Colonel Loss said, "The German people must decide their own fate."

He had served in Magdeburg during the 1970s and said he still was in touch with old East German friends, who were not particularly happy about developments. Some had lost their jobs, and others were worried that they, too, would be out of work. Some had been members of Stasi, he said, which accounted for their anxiety.

Igor was pleased about reunification although at that moment the mood of the former East German population was against the Soviet army. "Before the turn of events, people were forced to suppress their feelings. After the change, all feelings came to the surface." When Igor had been on a short assignment in East Germany in 1989 he was able to go everywhere in uniform. "Now it is dangerous," he said.

Colonel Loss confirmed this point and told about his wife's experience. While she was in the former East Berlin, a woman insulted and then pursued her. He was sorry that "Russians—Go Home" signs appeared after reunification. "Now women are worried about leaving the garrison alone. Some even refuse to send their children to the Pioneer camp because of a series of incidents with skinheads who taunted campers," he said.

Such groups killed seven Soviets, Colonel Loss said, and there were more than thirty incidents in which Soviet citizens were attacked and harassed, and women were raped. "Why doesn't the Western press report this?" he complained.

I did not want to get into an unpleasant discussion that would have challenged his insinuation that the Western press was anti-Soviet. But I could not imagine that the liberal, free press in Germany would pass up such headline stories if his information were accurate.

"Who has the right to leave the garrison?" I asked. He answered, "Soldiers who are drafted must remain in the garrison almost the whole time. On Sundays they are free to take group tours accompanied by an officer. Privates are not permitted to leave the garrison alone. Officers and their families have home leave and can visit the former East Germany, but based on the reunification treaty, they may visit West Berlin only on official business or by invitation."

"Now there are no border controls, and it would be easy to visit the West in civilian attire," I said. "That is a risk," he said and then described a theoretical situation, involving an automobile accident and the unpleasant consequences that could result if the police arrived.

Olga was permitted to accompany her husband when his orchestra played in West Berlin, and she and Igor spoke about the warm reception West Germans always extended to them. During the discussion it was clear that my conversation partners felt much more comfortable with their former "enemy" than with their "socialist brothers."

The 550,000 Soviet citizens living in what had been East Germany were scheduled to return to the Soviet Union no later than 1994, according to the Soviet-German treaty. This date could be changed, Colonel Loss pointed out, if living quarters for an estimated 36,000 officers' families were not completed by that date. This still left 19,000 families without homes—the Soviets would have to build dwellings.

Olga and Svetlana already had apartments in the Soviet Union and so the housing problem that concerned others did not affect them. They were busy calculating how their deutsche mark purchases would make their lives easier when they returned. Svetlana said cheerfully, "I am an optimist. When we return to Lvov next year I believe things will be better." Olga said thoughtfully, "We are far away from the problems at home. I am uncertain what awaits us." Quietly I added, "When you leave this Soviet paradise and return home, a shock awaits you." Everyone nodded and looked down.

7

THE LONELY
FIGHTER

*K*OLYA SURVIVED seventeen grueling months in prison, but he did not have the strength to fight against a system that tried again and again to kill his initiative and will to work. At the peak of his career, as an owner of one of the most popular private restaurants in Moscow, he gave up.

We had met through mutual Russian friends in 1980, when his wife, Vera, was a teacher of Persian at a branch of the prestigious Moscow University. At that time their three adorable children were under ten. The welcoming and warm family atmosphere reminded me of home, and whenever I was lonely I would visit these friends, who became as close to me as my own relatives.

Sometimes Vera would ask me to baby-sit, and the children and I considered the occasion a holiday. We would invent new dishes to make with the limited choice of ingredients, visit the Beriozka bookstore where the children could select Russian books (sold only for foreign currency), and then giggle half the night. Unlike many other Soviet children, Liuda, Irushka, and Alyosha had a model upbringing. At an early age Vera had taught them to shop, cook, do household chores, and take care of each other. They were also well mannered and unspoiled.

The children were a good physical mixture of their father and mother. Kolya was an attractive Mediterranean type with dark curly hair, a slightly curved thin nose, and narrow cheekbones. The dimple in the middle of his chin stood out when he smiled, and that was often. He was Assyrian and Vera was Russian, which was evident by her broad round face and wide nose, which she complained about. Her mother was Assyrian, but Vera decided to take her father's nationality. She knew that being registered as a Russian on her Soviet passport would make life easier.

In 1915 her grandparents fled from the oppression against Assyrians in Iran and arrived in the Soviet Union as poor refugees. Vera's mother had little schooling, which was not unusual for an Assyrian woman at that time. According to their tradition a woman's place is the home. The Assyrian community is tightly knit, and contact between Russian men and Assyrian women was then strictly forbidden. Vera's mother, however, violated the taboo.

While she was buying winter felt boots at the market, she met her future Russian husband. "Mother told us about their courtship," Vera said and then romantically described the situation. "He saw her long braid and beautiful face and followed her home, although she ignored him. Every day he stood patiently outside her house and waited for her to appear. She spoke only broken Russian, but this did not deter him. Finally he won her heart." Vera's mother knew that she would not be permitted to marry a Russian, and so they fled to another city to marry. From that day on she was ostracized by her family.

Soon after they married, her eighteen-year-old husband was recruited into the army, and she did not see him for the next six years. He was taken prisoner of war by the Germans and later was liberated by the Americans, which earned him the status of traitor at home. From the age of twenty-four until his death thirty years later, he was punished by not being given steady employment. The best he could do was to find part-time work, such as carrying freight and polishing shoes. His unhappiness led to alcoholism.

Meanwhile Vera's mother had four children and became practically the sole support of the family. She worked in a bread shop unloading bread and in a telephone office as a cleaning woman. She also took a job as a clerk in a food store so that she could feed her family. Fortunately her childless sister, who lived in Ukraine, helped out by sending fruit, meat, and vegetables to Moscow and inviting the children to spend their summer holidays with her. Vera recalled one summer in Ukraine when she, her sister, and two brothers ate so many strawberries that they broke out in a rash.

When I met Vera and Kolya, the food packages from Ukraine were still arriving, and the angelic aunt would come to Moscow to help Vera cook and care for the children. When both of us were in Moscow she prepared my favorite fish dishes and always gave me a jar of honey she had specially brought from her hometown. I could never refuse her gift and nicknamed her "Auntie Honey," the name family members have since adopted. "As poor as we were when we were first married we could buy more than we can buy today, such as cheese, butter, noodles, and sausage, which are scarce today," Vera said.

Vera grew up under difficult living conditions. For eighteen years she shared an unheated 24-square-meter [444-square-foot] room with her parents, two brothers, and a sister. In the morning they could not wash, Vera vividly recalled, because the water was frozen. Ice even formed under the carpet. "We did not have enough warm winter clothing and were constantly sick," she said. At a young age her brothers earned pocket money by delivering coal. "Often they came home with bloody hands," she said. Vera was more studious than her older brothers, so she had the windowsill to herself to do homework.

Her mother wanted the children to have a higher education, "although she did not know what a diploma was," Vera said. "She associated a university education with the elite. I could have worked as a hairdresser and earned much more than I do today, but she was opposed—she wanted me to be a doctor."

In the ninth and tenth grades Vera took medical courses in school, and once a week she was trained in a hospital. The conditions shocked her. "Dirt was everywhere. The nurses were often drunk from consuming rubbing alcohol intended for medical purposes. Patients' belongings were stolen," she said. When a nurse told her to give a patient an injection, Vera refused because she had no experience. The nurse said callously, "It makes no difference, he will die soon." Vera had associated the medical profession with compassionate and honest people in clean, orderly surroundings. After her disappointing experience in the hospital, she abandoned her plans to be a doctor.

She chose her profession purely by chance. Once, she saw three attractive and well-dressed young men singing melodious songs in an exotic language on a television program. They were students at the Institute for Oriental Languages. "At that time I was young and this type of man was my ideal," Vera said, and she decided that is where she would study and meet her future husband. Her mother had an Assyrian friend who worked at the institute, and she asked her to arrange a meeting between Vera and a docent. "That is a presumptuous idea. This institute accepts only the children of diplomats," the friend said and refused to help.

This did not discourage Vera. For the next two years she worked as a clerk at a medical institute to earn money for tutors who prepared her for the entrance exams in Russian, English, and literature. Through hard work and perseverance, Vera succeeded on her own and was accepted at the institute.

She was the only one in her class who came from a worker's family, but this did not affect her relations with fellow students. Before entering the institute she shared the prejudices of other working-class children, who thought the children of diplomats were spoiled and arrogant and that they would scorn someone from a different background. To her surprise her classmates seemed suited for the diplomatic profession. "They were intelligent, well mannered, and came from a milieu where harsh, vulgar language was not spoken. Their parents did not tell them, 'Go and buy vodka.' Instead, they discussed literature with their children and encouraged them to visit the theater, concerts, and art exhibitions."

Vera said that she had only one problem as a student. "When the others talked about theater life, actors and actresses, and recited poetry, I felt terribly ignorant and left out, but they respected me for my desire to learn. What I missed intellectually during my childhood I tried to make up for at the institute."

When Vera was twenty-two and in her fifth semester she married Kolya, whom she had met through relatives. At the time he was working as a locksmith, and she moved in with him in quarters that were even more humble than hers. The newlyweds lived in a tiny room in a cellar with a ceiling that was 5 feet 7 inches high. They were so poor that Vera had only one dress, and Kolya collected empty bottles to earn a few kopecks. With their first savings they bought a desk, which also served as a dining table. Her mother lent a hand by bringing them food, and his parents gave them money, which they put aside as a down payment for a one-room cooperative flat.

Vera was an excellent student. After five years at the institute she was assigned to teach Persian at the prestigious Academy of Foreign Trade. Her first salary was 157 rubles, and her last, before resigning seventeen years later, was only about 100 rubles more.

Their three children were born during the beginning of her teaching years, and she was one of the few mothers who took only two months' leave from work after the birth of each child. She was able to do this because her mother and close relatives helped out. Otherwise she would have had to remain home, like other mothers, for a year or more. Vera worked hard and was adored by her students, but when she was eligible for a promotion it was denied. At first she received no explanation. Then she was told the truth: One of her brothers had emigrated and the government regarded the relatives of emigrés with suspicion. Vera was not even permitted to join fellow teachers on business trips abroad.

When her sister married a foreigner and moved to France, Vera's life became even more difficult. The KGB questioned her students and even her nanny, but all had only words of praise for Vera. If she had not had three children, she would have been fired, she said.

After her colleagues learned that Vera had relatives living abroad, some avoided her. Most of those who did so were party members, who worried that contact with Vera would jeopardize their futures.

The Gorbachev era brought changes to her life. The liberalization of travel regulations permitted her to visit her brother and sister abroad, and her children were allowed to join her. The contrast between their world and the Western world was a shock at first. They visited me in Germany in 1990, and I remember how surprised Vera was that people were polite to each other and that there were no policemen standing on the streets.

At that time fourteen-year-old Irushka and seventeen-year-old Liuda were studying at one of the most exclusive schools in Moscow—a school that was often shown to foreign delegations. Vera and Kolya, like the other parents, had gained admittance for their children through connections and gifts. Many of the pupils were children of intellectuals and the *nomenklatura,* and the school was known for its excellent English instruction, progressive teachers, and modern facilities, such as a swimming pool.

After glasnost began, the English teachers used critical articles out of the English version of the liberal newspaper *Moscow News* for class discussions, instead of the uninspiring English texts that lauded the achievements of Lenin. Liuda's class was even permitted to read Solzhenitsyn.

When Liuda went on to medical school a few years later, she complained about the textbooks being old and boring. Although she was an excellent student like her mother, Vera had to give a bottle of cognac to one of Liuda's teachers so that she would give Liuda a passing grade.

Liuda said that perestroika had brought some positive changes for students. If they were dissatisfied with a teacher, they could go to the dean to complain or criticize the teacher directly. During one of her classes the students told the teacher, "What you have assigned us to read is much different from life. We want to read the truth." Many of her classmates even refused to attend the compulsory political course in which the works of Marx and Lenin were studied.

Irushka was not as good a pupil as her sister, Liuda, and when she failed the exams in the exclusive English school, she had to transfer to another. In the new school the majority of students were from working-class families, and she soon felt more comfortable in these surroundings. In her former school her classmates would smoke or sell Western clothing and cigarettes in the school bathroom. "They were even interested in the make of car that brought me to school," Irushka said. Emigrating to the United States and traveling abroad were the most popular topics of discussion. In the new school her classmates had no such interests, which was a relief to Irushka.

Her only complaint about her new school was the use of old-fashioned teaching methods and outdated textbooks. One of her teachers, who was in her sixties, still defended Stalin and Lenin and the leading role of the party. Irushka had nothing against the party. Her father was a Communist, she said.

Irushka's comments led to a long discussion with Kolya about the party. He had joined the party after completing his studies, he said, but he did not believe in communism. "It simply gave me professional advantages," he said. "Without party membership I would have had no chance of being promoted to a leading position."

Kolya had been born in Ukraine at the end of World War II and was the oldest of three brothers. His father was a shoemaker, who also held part-time evening jobs to support the family. Kolya was very clever with his hands, and by fourteen he had earned a reputation as a skilled, hard worker. His first part-time job was as a locksmith, and then he was employed as a carpenter while he still was attending school.

After completing ten grades he worked in a metal foundry and then in a machine-building factory, until he was recruited into the army. Upon his return he went to Moscow where he found still other kinds of work, such as plumbing and building roofs.

He married at the age of twenty-four and decided to continue his education in order to improve his job opportunities. During the day he did menial work, such as sorting and carrying vegetables and fruit, and in the evening he studied the technology of food preparation. Kolya was not a particularly good student, but Vera helped him pass his exams. He graduated in 1975 with a diploma as an engineer in the food industry.

At that time Moscow was beginning to prepare for the 1980 Olympics. Preparations included not only building new hotels but also repairing buildings that would serve as cafés, restaurants, and discotheques. Kolya was selected to oversee the renovation of a new café, and upon its completion he was named its director. I often brought friends to his café, where the tasteful decorations, good service, and polite waiters distinguished it from many other eating places in Moscow. "That period of my life was exciting and creative," Kolya said. "I handpicked a hard-working team, and the employees were give the chance to work under the best conditions."

During the Olympics the café was a showpiece for important foreign delegations. The employees even received bonuses, certificates of praise, and a medal from the Olympic Committee for their first-class service. When the Olympics were over, a reporter from *Moskovskaia pravda* visited Kolya's café and told him, "I want to write a story about this well-known café, but have not yet decided whether I will write a positive or negative article."

"This remark enraged me," Kolya said, "and I threw him out. I could not imagine that he could find any reasons to write anything negative about us." The journalist then began to visit the café regularly and search for its shortcomings. He wrote a series of articles, copies of which Vera showed me, in which he criticized the waiters for bad service and the kitchen for unsanitary conditions; he also accused Kolya of bribery. Vera explained that this journalist made it a practice to take bribes from directors and then write laudatory articles about their establishments even if the food and service were poor. If a proprietor refused to give him a bribe (as Kolya did), he would seek revenge by writing lies about the restaurant. "As a result of these articles, many people in the food business in Moscow were fired," she said.

After the first scathing article, Kolya refused to resign; but by the fourth article he admitted defeat. He found a job for a year as a technician; then he was asked to be the director of a factory that was responsible for feeding 30,000 workers in other factories.

All of this occurred at the time Gorbachev came to power in 1985. "Everything was unclear then. We did not know who he was or in what direction he would lead us. He was like a breath of fresh air. He spoke differently from his predecessors, and his ideas about glasnost and perestroika were appealing. In order to consolidate his power he brought in his own people, and a new epoch began." Party functionaries wanted to demonstrate their achievements in order to retain their positions, and they waged a campaign against the so-called trade Mafia. These were the directors of cafés and enterprises that sold food and consumer goods. After twenty-six directors of restaurants were arrested for bribery and other illegal practices, Kolya's life took a tragic turn.

On October 11, 1985, Kolya received a call from a KGB agent who invited him to a meeting that day. "I was not afraid," he said, "because I knew I had done nothing wrong. I did not have foreign currency and had never done anything against the Soviet government. I had relatives who lived abroad, but this was not a crime."

During the first part of the meeting, the KGB examining officer asked Kolya about himself and his work; then three other agents entered the room. They asked Kolya to join them, and soon he was being driven to the KGB building of the Russian Republic, where papers for his arrest awaited him.

"When two people denounce a person, he can be arrested," Kolya later said. "It was like 1937, when no evidence was necessary to arrest a man," Vera added. One of his two accusers was a militia man who worked in a division of the Ministry of Interior that was responsible for investigating economic crime. The second was his superior, who claimed Kolya had bribed him.

On the same day Vera was called out of her class and told to return home where people were waiting to speak with her. KGB agents greeted her and spent the next seven hours searching every nook and cranny of her apartment for incriminating evidence. They were looking for diamonds and foreign currency, but they found nothing, Vera said. At the end of the day they compiled a list of practically every object in the flat, from silverware to books, and warned her that every item might be confiscated.

This was of no interest to Vera. She only wanted to know where Kolya was. One of the twelve agents took pity on her and gave her a telephone number. "You can call this number and ask about your husband. If he does not come home today, he will not return at all," he said. Vera became hysterical, and Liuda, who was then thirteen, tried to calm her. "What has he done wrong?" she cried. No one could answer that question.

After his arrest Kolya was taken to a militia station, where he was forced to sleep on the wooden floor of a cell next to drug addicts and alcoholics for seven miserable days. During this time he was not permitted to shave or wash. "Even worse," he told me later, "I did not have any cigarettes."

His next call was in the Petrovka prison where the conditions were slightly better. Although he was questioned four to five times a day, he was at least given a mattress and water. The interrogators wanted Kolya to admit that he had bribed others and to denounce friends. His unwavering denials and intermittent silences resulted in threats against him. One interrogator said he could be shot. Another said he would never see his wife and children again, which was a cruel punishment for Kolya, an unusually devoted father and husband.

During the first fifteen months of Kolya's pre-trial detention, Vera was not permitted to have any personal contact with her husband, but she could send him one package a month. During this time I came to Moscow frequently to comfort Vera and could not help noticing that she had aged. She started dyeing her hair, which had suddenly turned gray, but she could not conceal the deep shadows under her eyes and the worry lines on her forehead. She had even lost her sense of humor and ability to laugh. Later she said to me, "Those seventeen months shortened my life by seventeen years."

I was often present when she painstakingly put together Kolya's package at the end of each month. At first she was told that articles such as soap, socks, and shirts were not included in the strict 5-kilo limit. Later everything was weighed together, and so she focused only on food. She dried bread and removed the rind from cheese so they would weigh less. When there was no sausage in shops I would buy some for Kolya from a Beriozka shop. Later Kolya said the prison food was so disgusting that he existed almost entirely from these "care" packages, and the 10 rubles Vera was permitted to send him every month. With this money he bought cookies, cigarettes, and sugar in the prison store; sometimes he could also purchase cheese and butter.

During those painful months Vera showed me copies of the letters she wrote to newspapers, writers, and government officials, including Gorbachev, in her fight for justice. "My husband is innocent and should be released," she pleaded. She then waited impatiently for a reply. To her frustration, each answer was the same. "We have examined your complaint and have sent it on to the government attorney of the Russian Republic."

Later Kolya said that the government attorney told him, "I hate you and your wife." No doubt, his anger stemmed from the bombardment of inquiries from the numerous officials to whom Vera had written. In spite of setbacks Vera did not give up. She visited the examining judge, hoping that she could win his sympathy; but this effort was also in vain.

For the first nine months Kolya had no right to his own attorney, and the only information Vera received about him was from an official who intentionally lied. He told her that her husband had quit smoking at a time when cigarettes were more important to him than food.

It was a blessing that Vera did not know about her husband's living conditions. He shared a cell with five other prisoners that had an open toilet in the middle and no fresh air. Once a day he was permitted to take a one-hour walk in a confined area. Then he was moved to another cell that was like a "sardine can," Kolya said. Sixty prisoners were assigned to space that thirty were officially permitted to occupy. "We lay so close to one another at night that we could turn over only when the order was given," he said. His cellmates were murderers and thieves as well as cooperative owners and people in commerce like himself. Arrested party officials and militia members were kept together in another cell so that they would not be murdered by the other prisoners. "The situation was too horrible and cruel to describe," Kolya said. Then he added, "The most awful part of this humiliating experience was the feeling that I was no longer a human being. I stopped believing in anything."

He whiled away his time listening to the radio and reading party newspapers to which he could subscribe. He also was drawn into discussions about perestroika, the favorite theme of his cellmates. Each hoped that the politics of Gorbachev would lead to his release. If this did not help, Kolya reckoned that he would be given at least a ten-year sentence for his alleged crime.

The prisoners could also order books from the prison library, and each could keep a book for ten days. This gave Kolya a choice of sixty books to read during that period. Card playing was also allowed, and often Kolya won and was rewarded with sugar.

According to the law, after nine months of pre-trial detention, a prisoner should have an official hearing to determine his guilt or innocence. When Kolya's time came, the Moscow courts were so full that he was eventually taken to a court in a city 800 kilometers away. Fifteen months after Kolya's arrest, the first trial took place, and Vera was permitted to sit across from him, though a window separated them. They could communicate only by telephone. "His face was yellow, and I was convinced he had tuberculosis," she said. "He had lost at least 20 kilos [44 pounds] and looked like an old man."

During the first court proceedings the accusing witnesses, whose number had grown from two at the time of his arrest to six, criticized the examining judge for forcing them to testify against Kolya. They also withdrew their charges that Kolya had bribed them with money, *pelmeni* (Russian ravioli), and meat. They apologized to him in court.

"This was not the first time that falsified evidence was used against a person," Kolya later remarked. "The witnesses were simply afraid," he said in an understanding tone. He spoke about a woman prisoner who refused to give false testimony and was threatened with being sent to an insane asylum where she would spend the rest of her life. Following further torture, she was raped, and then she tried to commit suicide. "This is what happens to people who refuse to make false statements," Kolya said.

"In this country those who give bribes as well as those who receive them are subject to arrest. At the same time power is based on bribes and payoffs," Kolya said. "If you want to get anything done, from repairing a faulty electric switch at home to replacing a motor in a factory elevator, you have to bribe someone." He then made a remark that I had often heard. "In this system it is impossible to work honestly. Corruption and bribery begin at the top and work their way down. The higher the official, the more he demands."

At that point Vera added, "People do not know any other method of working. I have friends with contacts in different stores. Through this network I can buy products, but naturally the salespeople expect a bribe in exchange for their services. In the eyes of the law everything that costs more than 5 rubles, from candy to flowers, can be regarded as a bribe and is punishable."

After two court proceedings Kolya was found innocent, and he was released on February 23, 1987, seventeen months after his arrest. Within an hour after his return Vera called and insisted that I come immediately. She didn't give a reason, and fearing the worst, I rushed to her apartment. Kolya opened the door and smiled with the old smile that I had missed for such a long time. I embraced him and burst into tears.

A few weeks later Kolya returned to his former position as director of the food factory. He also received all of his back pay, amounting to about 6,000 rubles. With this money and additional financial help from relatives, who had supported Vera during the trying months, he bought a car.

The economic changes that had taken place recently gave him hope that the centralized planning system would soon be abolished, and workers and employees would finally be able to participate in the decision-making process. "When an employee is constantly given orders and has no feeling of responsibility, he becomes lazy, indifferent, and careless," Kolya said. "My dream is to have my own business and demonstrate what I can do."

The enactment of a law in 1986 permitting cooperatives—private businesses—gave Kolya this opportunity. After discussing with me and others his idea to set up a private restaurant that featured international cuisine, he embarked on the complicated road of receiving permission. The bureaucratic obstacles were enormous, but he was fortunate to meet a Moscow official who knew his history and was willing to support his application.

The government gave him a 20,000-ruble credit and for three months he and other laborers worked around the clock to renovate the rat-infested, crumbling building he was assigned. His skills as a handyman were useful in solving construction problems that would have otherwise delayed the completion of the restaurant by months, if not years.

Kolya decided on the menu only after consulting with cooking experts from various countries. Eventually a French friend, whose hobby was cooking, came to Moscow to work with Kolya's Soviet cooking team for one month. The cook suggested a menu of dishes that could be prepared using only local products.

One month after the restaurant opened in spring 1988, it was so popular that tables had to be reserved in advance. One year later it was expanded to include a terrace, where at least fifty guests could sit comfortably in the shadow of trees. Foreign and Soviet newspapers wrote about the restaurant's excellent kitchen and service, and Kolya received letters of praise and thanks from distinguished foreigners who had spent a lovely evening in his restaurant. His success was followed by invitations to attend culinary events in America and France.

The restaurant was no sooner in operation than racketeers demanded a piece of the action. They asked Kolya for 25,000 rubles "protection money." If he refused they would burn down his restaurant. "No cooperative or joint venture can stay in business in Moscow without paying off racketeers," Kolya said. He hired his own group of bodyguards from the north Caucasus, and the problem with racketeers was resolved. "The gangsters even pay for their meals when they eat here," Vera said in a serious tone.

Kolya's business was booming, and he was earning about 1,000 rubles a month, which permitted Vera to give up her work at the institute and become a full-time housewife. He had plans to open other restaurants with friends, when the first blow came from the government. During the summer of 1990 new tax laws were introduced requiring cooperatives to pay, in some cases, as much as 65 percent of their profit. The next shock was Gorbachev's decree that gave security squads from the KGB and the Ministry of the Interior the right to enter government enterprises, joint ventures with foreign firms, and cooperatives without a search warrant and to carry out audits of their wares, cash holdings, and accounts. The official reason for this directive was to wipe out the black market and fight economic irregularities.

"It is impossible to work in this country without violating laws that are intentionally unclear and open to interpretation by those with decisionmaking power," Kolya said. "I have no clearly defined rights as a citizen, and I am afraid that a new wave of arrests might take place. I do not want to be a victim of a corrupt system again. At this moment I have everything I need—healthy children, an adoring wife, friends, a comfortable apartment, and challenging work. I cannot understand why the government always tries to destroy what is good. We desperately need the growth of free enterprise, which is our only hope. I have never believed in communism, which is only an ideology on paper. I always believed in hard work. A man who wants to work honestly has no place here."

Kolya's resignation made me worry; I was concerned that I might not see one of my favorite Russian families when I next came to Moscow.

8

THE LAST COMMUNIST

L ENA AND I called Anatoly "the last honest Communist." During the twenty-eight years he was a party member, he was "a true believer, even a fanatic," his wife said. I knew many party members, but no one was as loyal and full of principles as Anatoly.

Before I lived in Moscow I had a stereotyped image of a Communist: He had a broad fleshy face with a sinister expression. In public he wore a dark hat with a narrow brim. Anatoly was just the opposite, and I had to change my impression. He was slight, attractive, and had a winning smile. The only hat I ever saw on his head was the plaid English cap I brought him from England.

Lena was stunning with short gray hair and penetrating dark eyes. Her nose, cheeks, and lips were finely chiseled and her skin showed years of tender care. Lena was a health addict who jogged every morning, took cold showers, and treated her skin to vitamin baths. Her special formula was ice cubes, cucumbers, yogurt, egg yolks, honey, and strawberries. She encouraged me to follow her physical fitness routine and to take better care of my skin, but I was too lazy and thought nature should take its course. Anatoly and Lena balanced each other temperamentally. She was emotional and outspoken. He was reserved and soft-spoken, but when he said something, it was worth listening to.

"I never wanted to join the party," Lena said, "but that does not mean that I am unpatriotic. I love my motherland and will never leave it." Lena came from a family that was repressed during the 1930s. She remembered hearing stories when she was young about the political leaflets her grandmother concealed in her sewing machine and about her grandfather's arrest in 1937. Her grandmother searched for her husband in Siberia, but she died without finding him. Lena, fearing political repercussions because her parents were also considered traitors, did not continue the search. Only after the death of her parents and following a 1986 change in policy that revised their status as traitors did Lena resume the search for her grandfather. She wrote a letter to the Office of the Public Prosecutor and learned that her grandfather had been shot in 1938 for joining a so-called counterrevolutionary conspiracy.

"My parents were not supporters of the system that made their lives miserable." Lena's father was fifty-one when he married Lena's mother, a Muscovite, and brought her to Siberia, his birthplace. Lena recalls the great love her parents had for each other and used them as a model for her life. Her mother was a teacher, and her father was a boat pilot. Together they earned 160 rubles a month, which was enough to live on very modestly. "I never had beautiful toys or clothes, but I was happy," she said. When she was in her early teens she dreamed of earning a lot of money. She would then drink hot chocolate every morning, own a tape recorder, and listen to all of the Strauss waltzes.

Anatoly also came from a humble background and spent his early years living with his grandmother in a village. "We both were unspoiled and grew up with a deep sense of responsibility," Lena said. "This is probably the main thread that binds us today. It also creates problems for us professionally. Often people shirk responsibility in order to retain their job rather than stand up for what they believe and face the consequences."

Lena's parents had been believers and imbued her with strong moral principles. As a student she was indignant that party members, such as the first party secretary, used their position to reap benefits. Why did he have the right to buy a car while others had to wait in line for years, she asked? She also criticized other injustices. Why were Communist functionaries given priority over others to travel abroad? Why did they have job opportunities that were denied to those with better qualifications? Why could they decide the fate of non-party members?

"I saw the significant difference between Communists holding power and ordinary party members, like Anatoly," Lena said. Those in good positions could take a vacation in a Central Committee sanitorium where every family member had a separate room and bathtub. "Is this equality?" Lena asked her husband, the loyal Communist. "I have everything I need," Anatoly said in his usually calm voice.

I met Lena, Anatoly, and their son Sergei at the end of the 1970s when Anatoly was working as a journalist in Yakutsk. He had volunteered for the assignment in Siberia because he was a romantic who loved nature. He also wanted to be a writer. In Siberia he earned twice as much as in Moscow and he could save for his future career. The geographical distance also helped him to view Moscow differently. At the same time he discovered a new, unknown land, he said. During his years in Siberia he reported about the extreme living and working conditions in the Soviet Far East and wrote two books about his travels. The highlight of his experience was meeting Lena, his Russian wife, who was born in Yakutsk, like Sergei.

A kayak trip with Anatoly, Sergei, and Lena in Siberia cemented our friendship. We all loved nature, and it was nice to forget about politics. Lena and I were the extroverts, and the men were the introverts. We were great talkers and they were good listeners. We overflowed with emotion, and they with levelheadedness.

After ten years in Siberia Anatoly and his family returned to Moscow, his hometown, and the three moved into a room, measuring 12 square meters, in a communal flat. This had been Anatoly's home during his bachelor days. Lena's first three years in Moscow were very unhappy, and she often wished that she were back in Yakutsk. She and her neighbor quarreled. She had to live out of cartons. She spent three hours every day commuting to and from work. Big city life and the Moscow mentality depressed her. I was embarrassed whenever she visited me in my five-room apartment. I had so much living space and she so little.

Lena would have been pleased if Anatoly had bribed someone or used his connections to improve their living situation, but he staunchly refused. That meant they would probably have to wait years before being assigned a new flat. Anatoly's father began to ail, and the doctor said he had terminal cancer and had to be taken care of. Anatoly and Lena therefore decided to exchange both flats for one large flat. They were fortunate to find a three-room apartment in the center of the city. It was in shabby condition, like the run-down building in which it was located, but this did not trouble Anatoly. He and Lena would make the major repairs themselves. Every weekend for the next six months they worked on the apartment's face-lift. The streaks of paint on the wall in the corridor are a vivid reminder of my contribution.

Lena's first job in Moscow was as a translator at the Gas Institute. She had studied English and had been an interpreter for foreign visitors in Yakutsk. Anatoly joined the staff of one of the ultra-conservative party newspapers and later switched to the trade union newspaper, where his job was more interesting.

The editor of this newspaper was a Central Committee appointee, and Anatoly's critical articles did not always please his boss. When Anatoly found fault with a director of an institute, the article was not published. Other articles were cut, and his interview with Boris Yeltsin was shelved for eight months.

A new journalistic challenge then presented itself. A politburo member encouraged journalists of the central press to go to the provinces to revive the local press, and Anatoly packed his bags again. He went to Adzhaira, Georgia, where he spent three months writing about housing problems. The local citizens were eager to air their complaints to a Moscow journalist. Anatoly learned from them that the best housing was being built for party leaders. He wrote about the situation, which displeased local authorities; they complained to the Central Committee. Once again his articles were cut.

At the end of 1988 Anatoly began to believe in perestroika even though he "saw how the press lied and how helpless I was until then," he said. "The people started to awaken, and I decided it was impossible to accept the system the way it was and continue to be silent." He declared himself a candidate for political office. Honest journalism was his motto, and his constituency elected him as a deputy to the Moscow city council. This gave him a platform to publicize his views about unjust party politics.

During this period I noticed a transformation in Anatoly. His strong, determined face looked haggard and gray. The lines in his cheeks became grooves. He was always trim, but now he was only skin and bones. He developed a nervous habit of clearing his throat. Speaking seemed to be an effort. When he came home, he would eat quickly and then disappear into his study where he read until the early morning hours.

Anatoly shared his conflict with Sergei, who was serving his obligatory term in the army, and Sergei wrote a concerned letter to his mother. "Father asked me what to do—to remain in the party or to leave it. I do not know. I am not a party member, but I said to him, leave it as you leave the land which is infertile. Leave it as you leave a swamp where there is nothing more than quag, duckweed, sedge, and decaying trees. Leave it! You have done everything you could do for it, and it has sucked all the juices out of you. For years people have entered the party to make a career for themselves. That was never your mistake. Leave it!"

In July 1990 Anatoly took the most painful step in his life. He resigned from the party. A day later he was named editor-in-chief of *Kuranty,* an independent weekly newspaper whose sponsor was the Moscow city council. This newspaper gave him the platform to vent his rage against the injustices of the system. The newspaper was vehemently anticommunist and even won the dubious distinction of being criticized by Gorbachev. A Central Committee order for the party press to attack *Kuranty* allegedly followed. This helped to boost the newspaper's popularity, and it started appearing daily.

"Nobody publishes such politically sharp and critical material today," he said proudly. "The task of journalists is to analyze and criticize everything, no matter who is in power. I do not know any limits to criticism." This irritated some of his readers, who accused *Kuranty* of being yellow press. Others admitted that many articles were worth reading, but the anticommunist and anti-Gorbachev line were too extreme. Anatoly conceded that his newspaper was anticommunist but only in the sense that "we are against their ideology," he said. "Two years ago I understood that a multiparty system is the only way to real democracy. I am not against the existence of the Communist party, as long as it does not violate the constitution. The purpose of *Kuranty* is to tell people about other ideologies, parties, social trends, and what is being born in the country. Freedom of the press is what I practice in my newspaper."

Anatoly's decision to leave the party seemed to purge him, and he appeared more relaxed and communicative. But he worked a fifteen-hour day and Lena felt neglected and lonely. She was employed at the Soviet AIDS foundation and was an untiring and energetic worker, but this was only a part of her life. She also missed Sergei.

Their apartment was only a ten-minute bus ride away from mine, and I made an effort to see more of Lena in order to cheer her up. We also had a lot in common. Sometimes I would be drinking tea in the kitchen when Anatoly returned from work shortly before midnight, and he would join us to unwind. He often had the next day's newspaper in hand and would talk excitedly about its sensational contents.

On a few occasions Anatoly discussed his past and his former disillusionment. "I grew up a full-blooded Stalinist like millions of Soviet people who were also fooled by our ideology. I was an active Komsomol member—a Communist organization for teenagers—and the Communist ideology was life for me. I did not propagate ideology. I advocated an honest way of life and fought against injustice. It did not occur to me to criticize the party leadership. I believed that Sakharov and dissidents were anti-Soviet men because that is what our media said. I never read what they wrote because I thought they had betrayed their country. Now I understand that they were much wiser than I."

Previously I had avoided discussing politics with Anatoly. I was afraid that our diametrically opposed views would jeopardize our relationship. When he supported the Afghanistan invasion, saying, "It defended the interests of the country," I could no longer be silent. Lena supported me and said, "I understood at once that our boys were sacrificing their lives for nothing in Afghanistan." Later Anatoly changed his mind.

Anatoly had formerly supported all decisions of his government and was convinced that communism was the only path his country should follow. It was people who spoiled the system, he said, and he began a campaign against dishonest Communists. "If a worker pointed out a bad director, I wrote about the director. I responded to people's complaints and this made them believe the system was more or less just."

When the mass media started telling the truth about achievements in the West—the high standard of living, the benefits for the poor and unemployed—Anatoly began to have doubts. He buried himself in translations of Western publications, and my copies of *Time* and *Newsweek* provided Lena and him with night reading. He learned that the union can protect a worker against his boss in the West. "In this country no one can protect himself against the state," he said. "I understand that the exploitation of man in a capitalist society is often terrible, but it is not as terrible as exploitation of man in a socialist state."

Anatoly also read up on subjects such as the military, which had formerly been classified for journalists. "In the 1960s we were far behind the United States in armaments, but between 1975 and 1978 we reached parity. This was at the expense of the people, who received goods of inferior quality. The high-quality material was allocated for missiles, tanks, and machine guns, but God save us from making knives for the masses out of the military's precious titanium or good aluminum alloys. We launched rockets that were not worse than yours, but we could not make a quality tape recorder. The party is the greatest anti-Soviet organization in the country," Anatoly said. "It has been robbing people like me for years."

This reminded me of a heated conversation he had had with Lena years earlier. She was in need of a winter coat, but they could not afford it because Anatoly had to pay high party dues after receiving an honorarium for his book. "Why were my party dues three times more than my union dues? The union gives me vouchers for my holiday, and it pays for my sick leave. The party gives me nothing. The party has always been saying it was a protector of the people, supposedly defending their interests. In reality it does not give a damn about them. The party must be plunged into such conditions where it will be a real party. The Communist party today is not any more than a state structure."

In the cities I visited, the party building stood out for its size and pomposity. The party also had its own clinics, hotels, sanatoriums, and cars. In Moscow, next to old apartment buildings, which are fire hazards, stand new apartment houses with elevator operators and security guards. These buildings are reserved for higher functionaries and their families, who have five times more space than the official norm. At the same time they pay less rent than those living in smaller quarters.

"Gorbachev is the best leader of our nation since the revolution. He felt he could build a just society, but the Communist ideology isn't suitable for a just society. I do not want Gorbachev to resign. Let him remain as president and reign like the Queen of England. According to dialectics, everything that has been created has to die sometime. During the disintegration process it is useless to interfere. We have to let the Soviet Union and the Communist party die quietly. There is no need to resuscitate what is impossible to resuscitate. The president must plan for the future after the Union collapses and the party loses power. He understands that democratic opposition is gaining power through strikes and demonstrations, but the opposition is too weak to come to power at the union level. Gorbachev has shown that he can tolerate criticism and is willing to make compromises. Our only hope for the future is to strengthen the power of the republics. In this way the reorganization of society will be made peacefully."

9

THE STRIKING DEMOCRATS

*M*INERS IN SIBERIA and in other parts of the country were the first to respond to Boris Yeltsin's call for a national strike after the coup in August 1991. Since July 1989, a historic month in the lives of many Soviet miners, they became known as the branch of the working force that was willing to fight for their rights in the Soviet Union. At that time they went on strike to demand better living and working conditions. After the first strike others followed, and my interest in the miners grew. This group, I thought, could eventually paralyze the economy.

My friends Anatoly and Lena agreed with me, and on one memorable evening Lena spontaneously proposed that we visit miners in the Kuzbass, an area rich in coal in western Siberia. She knew a correspondent who lived there, and she could ask him to make arrangements for us. I accepted the proposal immediately, mainly because Lena would be accompanying me. The last time we had traveled together was when we took a kayak trip in Siberia more than ten years earlier. At that time Anatoly, six-year-old Sergei, and their puppy, Shu-Shu, were present. This time just the two of us would be traveling together. Lena was able to take a week off from her job at the AIDS foundation, and we planned to visit in mid-November 1990 before the severe Siberian winter set in.

Our plane was scheduled to depart at 2 A.M., and in spite of Aeroflot's confirmation on the telephone that the plane would be leaving on time, we learned at the airport it would be delayed one hour. Explanations are usually not given for delays, so we sat impatiently waiting for our flight to be called. Two hours passed and still no word. The Aeroflot employees made an effort to find out the new time of departure, but received no information. Every hour we were told to wait yet another hour. Aeroflot finally came up with a plausible excuse: The airport in Moscow was closed because of fog. I believed this until I saw other planes landing and taking off a few hours later. The next explanation was that the plane's wings had to be de-iced. The third excuse was that the Novokuznetsk airport was closed because of bad weather.

During the long delay we whiled away our time in the special hall of Intourist, which caters to foreigners and is supposed to provide better service than Soviet citizens receive. It was true that the cafeteria sold oranges and rarities like cookies and chocolate. But the unsanitary conditions in the bathroom were no different from those in most public places. The toilets were overflowing, smelly, and, as usual, there was no toilet paper. The one and only wastebasket in the hall stood in the middle of a heap of debris.

We were lucky to find two hard-backed chairs in which we could doze while other passengers were forced to lean against the wall or stretch out on the floor. They ran the risk of being swept aside by an obese, sullen cleaning woman on night duty who seemed to derive special satisfaction from yelling at the sleeping passengers who obstructed her. If they were in the way of her vicious broom, she awakened them. Those who had thrown paper or cigarettes on the floor received a special reprimand. "You are not civilized," she roared. This remark provoked a lively argument with a chain-smoker. "In civilized Western countries the passengers are given a room in a hotel when the delay is long. Also they receive more exact information," he said. "That's a lie. The conditions are the same all over the world," she said confidently. And then she ended the discussion by repeating that he was uncivilized and calling him a few vulgar names.

A short visit to the noisy main hall with a sticky floor made me grateful to Intourist for its spacious, quiet waiting room. Soviet passengers and their mountains of baggage were lying everywhere. The unshaven faces and rumpled attire indicated that many had spent several days at the airport waiting for their flights. They had no other choice. Hotel rooms are not usually available to Soviets in transit.

After fifteen hours of waiting we were told that our flight would be postponed for an indefinite period of time. Exhausted and annoyed, we decided to cancel the trip, but on the way to reclaiming our luggage we heard an announcement on the loudspeaker saying our flight would be departing "immediately." Seventeen hours after we were supposed to take off, our plane left Moscow.

The passengers were in good spirits, and the man seated behind us offered us a full cup of cognac. When we refused, his friend gave us a pomegranate. They were both from Azerbaijan and were making their semi-annual business trip to Novokuznetsk. They had 15,000 flowers stored in the baggage compartment. I was concerned that the flowers would not survive the cold and delay, but they reassured me that the packaging protected them for four days. Later I heard that one tulip sold for 8 rubles at the private market.

The Aeroflot meal was the standard one I had been served as long as I could remember. It consisted of cold chicken that had acquired the nickname "rubber eagle," cold rice, stale brown bread, and fatty salami. The cookie was always the best part of the meal. Unfortunately the water in the economy-class toilet had frozen, and we were not permitted to use the toilet in first class.

The four-hour flight, which covered 3,000 kilometers and four time zones, brought us to Novokuznetsk in the wee hours of a windy, cold morning. Bus and taxi service would begin two hours later, at 6 A.M., so I decided to curl up on a comfortable bench in the hall for a little snooze. Lena did not want to wait any longer and went off to try to arrange a ride into town.

The quiet, unhurried atmosphere at the crowded Novokuznetsk terminal contrasted sharply with the Moscow airport. The local people were also friendlier and more polite here. Across from me sat a grinning teenager, who began talking to me. She was a university student in Moscow and had returned to her hometown, Novokuznetsk, to visit her mother, who worked in the hotel where she assumed we would be staying. She was studying economics and asked me first about joint ventures and then about unemployment in the West. "Is it true that a scientist has to work as a taxi driver in New York?" "Are Russian diplomas recognized abroad?" and so on.

A middle-aged woman with a fur hat that was almost as round as she was had been listening to the conversation and interrupted to say to the girl, "I am tired of young people who are looking only for comfortable jobs. They should learn to use their hands, not only their heads. I have worked my whole life, and youth should learn what it means to work. Young people think only about themselves and how to earn easy money. They buy goods at a low price and sell them at higher prices. Honest people cannot buy anything in a legal way today. There are plenty of jobs in the Soviet Union, but not the elite work you are looking for." She then walked off in a huff.

"She's crazy," the girl commented and continued talking, as though the conversation with the woman had not taken place. Wanting to be helpful, she warned me about the dangers that awaited me in Novokuznetsk. The hotel was full of capitalists and thieves, and I should not forget to lock my door. Under no circumstances should I go out on the streets alone at night. Fifty percent of the population are ex-convicts, who had served sentences in prisons in the area, and it was no wonder that the city was a bed of crime.

"I don't want to frighten you," she said, noticing the expression in my eyes, and then she resumed. "Mother told me that the racketeers and Mafia have gained a foothold in the city." She told me about a cooperative owner who had refused to sell his Japanese car to the Mafia; they burned down his garage with the car inside. The next incident involved a woman who had won a VCR in a lottery contest. She was forced to sell it to the Mafia for 500 rubles, which was less than 10 percent of its cost on the black market.

I was relieved to hear Lena's voice, which interrupted this unsettling description of life in Novokuznetsk. "Lois, grab your things and run." She had convinced a jeep driver, who had already picked up two other passengers, to wait for us. We squeezed into the remaining space and began the 35-kilometer drive to town. The sky was clear and the snow knee-deep. When we talked about our delay in Moscow because of the closed airport in Novokuznetsk the driver said, "The weather has been wonderful here." "Why did they lie to us in Moscow?" I whispered to Lena. The driver continued, "We have a national fuel shortage, and Aeroflot must cancel two or three flights daily from Moscow to Novokuznetsk." This explained why the majority of passengers who flew with us had tickets for flights that should have taken off a day-and-a-half earlier. I was suddenly grateful for being a privileged foreigner. As a Soviet citizen I would have had to wait at least thirty-six instead of seventeen hours at the airport.

The middle-aged couple in the jeep had just spent a week in Moscow and were glad to be home again. They complained about the empty shops and the high prices in the capital. In Novokuznetsk cheese and butter were available in state shops, they said proudly, and the price of meat at the private market was 8 rubles instead of 30. While we were talking, a policeman stepped out of a "GAI" station—a traffic control post—and flagged us down. He checked the driver's registration papers and waved us on, satisfied that the car was not stolen.

We had to awaken the hotel attendant, who had expected us the day before. Our exhausted faces earned us the best accommodations in the hotel, a suite with a bedroom and separate workroom with refrigerator. This was luxurious by Russian standards, and we did not refuse. It was 6 A.M. local time and 2 A.M. in Moscow. We had been awake almost two days, and Lena and I fell into the sleep of the dead, which ended too quickly.

The chairman of the miners' working committee was waiting to receive us at noon, and our tight schedule did not permit us to be late. His office was located in the ghost-like party building, whose corridors were empty. The only activity was in a small conference hall, where the working committee was conducting business. Our entrance stopped a heated discussion among a dozen men. The chairman greeted us. He then asked the men to stay and to participate in our discussion.

The head of the working committee was forty years old and had been a driver at a motor depot. During the first miners' strike in July 1989, he had led the strike committee in his department. Coal miners and his fellow workers joined forces with those in other factories and stopped working. Later he was elected to his present post.

The government pacified the miners by making many promises, but after it kept very few, they went on strike again and set up their own independent trade union. Previously the main function of the trade union was to pass on production orders from the party. The new trade union gave priority to the needs of the workers.

The chairman admitted that the strikes had accomplished little materially, but they boosted the miners' morale. The miners had been exploited like slaves. The word "slave" reminded me of a poster that hung in the office of the strike committee in Donetsk, the coal capital of Ukraine. It showed a Soviet worker in shackles; a ring around his neck was labeled "KGB," his iron belt was labeled "Propaganda," and the iron ball he carried was identified as the "Communist party of the Soviet Union." Below was the caption, "We have nothing to lose but our chains."

"Now the miners know they are human beings with rights, and by striking they are fighting for these rights," the chairman said. "They want economic independence, but they must understand that this is based on political changes."

Gorbachev had reacted to the first strike with encouraging words. "The workers are taking things into their own hands, and this inspires me greatly." While he praised the workers for displaying their zeal, the local authorities regarded the strike as a violation of work discipline, and they began a campaign to intimidate the workers. When the miners in one mine refused to go to work because they had no hot water, the administration docked their wages. This frightened those who had families to support, and they went back to work.

In the metallurgical plants, where the workers were poorly organized, some were fired and others were penalized. The administration played one worker against another by awarding scarce goods to those who demonstrated good behavior. In some enterprises the bosses attempted to bribe working committee members by offering them housing out of turn. This practice dated to the time when Communist party officials tried to boost party membership by promising apartments to prospective members.

The importance of the working committee became clear to me when two women, bundled in warm coats and fur hats, burst into the room and shouted that one of the members of the working committee had to come at once and establish order. They had been lined up in front of a store for two hours, waiting to purchase pillows with coupons. A half hour later the representative returned with a triumphant smile. "The people have lost faith in the ability of local authorities to settle their problems, and they have turned to us as the defender of their rights," the chairman said.

After listening to complaints about the deteriorating situation in mines and daily life, I asked, "What would you do if you were in Gorbachev's shoes today?" A miner was the first to respond. "I would reconstruct the plants and buy new technology. The equipment we presently use is worn out and dangerous. It is necessary to do away with the present centralized system, which puts us under pressure to fulfill the government plan at any cost. This leads to violations of safety regulations and accidents." A taxi driver, who was sitting at the table, said, "I would give the people food and clothing, and Russia sovereignty and self-government. The workers, not Moscow, should decide the production plan. The party must relinquish its authority." The chairman of the committee said, "All the plants and enterprises should belong to the workers. If we were free we could expand production, earn higher wages, and live better." An airline pilot who wandered in during our discussion said, "A law must be enforced that every citizen has equal rights in the country. Power must be in the hands of the municipal authorities who are elected by the people. We need stability and more power for the people."

Next on the agenda was an auto tour of the city and its outskirts, which was preferable to walking in the minus 30-degree gusts of wind. Later I learned that this wind saved the city from severe and deadly industrial pollution. As I sat in the comfort of the car, I felt sorry for those stamping their freezing feet at bus stops. They were dressed in warm thick coats and fashionable voluminous fur hats, but their chic Western boots were not made for this climate. Had they worn the unstylish rural felt boots that the grandmothers and grandchildren tramped in, they wouldn't have had cold feet.

A street several lanes wide ran through the center of the city; shops and drab-looking apartment buildings lined both sides. On the outskirts of the city we passed a red brick building about a block long, with towering impregnable walls. Its tiny windows with bars established its identity. The taxi driver said that this prison had been enlarged ten years ago; he added that its inmates were criminals who worked on road construction. "But no one has escaped for the past several decades," he said, to my relief.

Siberia is historically known for its prison camps, where prisoners provide a cheap labor force for constructing the railroad and roads. After criminals served their terms many remained in the area. This accounted for the high crime rate and alcoholism in the Kuzbass. In addition, the so-called undesirable elements who had formerly lived in Leningrad, Moscow, and other big cities were exiled to this area. To these groups belonged prostitutes and known troublemakers who were forced to leave Moscow shortly before the beginning of the Olympics in 1980.

Our driver was a wonderful guide, and he provided us with information that was not included in travel books, most likely because Novokuznetsk had so few foreign visitors. It is a working-class city with more than 600,000 residents. Forty-eight percent are employed in the metallurgical industry, in mining, and in the construction of roads, railroads, and buildings. The remainder are family members, students, and pensioners. Of the seventy major enterprises, twelve are mines, which employ more than 23,000 workers. Novokuznetsk has only two higher educational institutes: the Teachers Training Institute and the Metallurgical Institute.

"If we had more intellectuals living here, we would have more information about the frightening ecological state of our city," the driver said. "Our city is officially one of the five most endangered in the Soviet Union, but the environmental movement is very weak here. Our other problems—such as a shortage of food, clothing, medicine, housing, kindergartens, and low wages—take priority over the environment. The workers also worry about factories being closed due to obsolete equipment and unemployment. Everybody believes we will have time to think about ecology after we begin to live better."

While he was speaking we passed one factory stack after another that was belching black smoke, and I remembered that a French ecological group labeled this city as the dirtiest and most polluted in the Soviet

Union. Even I noticed the air pollution, which was irritating my throat and making me cough. The snow was as gray as my face and hands, and when I undressed that evening I noticed that my underwear was also gray.

"No child in this city is born healthy, and many suffer from leukemia," the driver said. To emphasize the health hazard he told us that the life expectancy in Novokuznetsk is between sixty-three and sixty-four, which is lower than most cities in the Soviet Union. Every third miner suffers from some kind of skin disease, but there are no special centers for the treatment of these diseases. The high incidence of lung and respiratory ailments, lung cancer, and other diseases results from the shameful neglect of the environment. The poisonous industrial air pollutes not only human lungs but also the water, soil, and food. The inadequate water purification system in Novokuznetsk causes a high incidence of hepatitis, and residents are told to boil the drinking water.

New multi-story apartment houses dotted the outskirts of town. They were near civilian living quarters built by German prisoners held after the end of World War II. Pointing to them, the driver said, "They are more than forty years old and are still the most attractive and comfortable buildings in the city." The soot-smudged faces of miners, returning from their shift, reminded me that a shortage of soap had been one of the gripes of the striking miners.

In the evening we were guests in a miner's flat that was certainly not typical. Nadya, our hostess, proudly showed us her spacious, tastefully furnished three rooms, which contained almost everything that a prosperous Russian family could purchase. Only a VCR was missing. The dark mahogany-colored wardrobe and cupboards fit in with the velvet-covered sofa and chairs. In a glass cabinet stood crystal vases and ornate dishes and bowls, which looked as though they were to be admired but not touched. The floors and walls were covered with brightly colored Mongolian carpets, which the family had bought in Mongolia, Nadya said. They had lived there for a few years.

As she shut the window, Nadya said, "We are used to sleeping with closed windows because the surrounding plants discharge a lot of harmful substances, especially at night." She apologized for her husband's absence, but she was certain that we three women would enjoy the evening without him. We chose to dine in the cozy, small kitchen, and while she set the table Nadya mentioned, for a reason I don't recall, that she was a party member. This piqued Lena's interest and became the main topic of the evening.

She began with the cutting remark, "I told Lois we would be visiting a poor miner's family, but we have landed in the lap of luxury." Nadya interpreted this as a compliment but, nevertheless, protested weakly. "We live like the average mining family," she said. "Then the miners had no reason to strike," Lena commented.

I realized that I would learn much more if I permitted the Siberian-born Lena to use her direct, no-nonsense style of speaking. If I had led the discussion, my politeness and tact would have left me mainly with food recipes and other such banalities. Only occasionally did I find it necessary to interrupt with an innocuous remark to cool down the atmosphere.

Lena and Nadya discovered that they had one thing in common. Both rose shortly after 5 A.M., did morning exercises, and took a cold shower. Then their lives took different paths. For the previous seventeen years Nadya's working day in the mine began at 8 A.M. and ended at 4 P.M. Today she had bought milk and tomatoes on the way home, but had no time to stand in the line for cheese. A friend had helped her by buying a cake for our dessert.

Lena asked Nadya if she could explain why there was a shortage of goods. She talked about the television broadcasts, that we had also seen in Moscow, of discarded and decaying meat and sausage. "Somebody is purposely doing this to make the situation in the country even worse. It is sabotage," she said. "We need discipline. Strict measures should be taken. I belong to the group that thinks Stalin's measures should be restored, but, of course, without murder and repression."

Lena remarked in a controlled tone, "In the United States and Germany order is maintained without an iron hand. They have strong parliaments, which defend the people's rights." Nadya ignored this comment and said, "Discipline is missing everywhere. Today the leaders are elected, instead of being appointed, and look at the result. The winners do not enforce discipline. If party people were elected a worker could not leave his working place before the end of the working day to settle his private business."

Lena provoked Nadya with the remark, "Since you don't suffer from poverty, your main demand is the restoration of order. What if the Mafia took over and promised that order would be restored?" "No, never the Mafia," Nadya said. "They are already in Novokuznetsk. Our shops are empty, and we are forced to buy clothes for black-market prices. Who can afford a pair of boots for 1,500 rubles?" For the unreflective Nadya, every clever businessman was a member of the Mafia.

Nadya remained resolute. "The guilty must be punished," she said. Lena tried to reason with her and pointed out if the shops were full of products of a good quality there would be no need for black marketeers. The cooperatives and black market fill the needs of the people, where the government has failed. "The system is at fault," Lena said, raising her voice.

Nadya changed the subject and said to our surprise that she supported the miners' strike. "For many years the authorities denied the miners their legal rights. The workers used to be afraid of the Party Committee, but the threat of punishment no longer intimidates them." This reminded me of a remark made by a young miner, "The grave doesn't scare me. I work in a tomb every day." (*New York Times*, April 14, 1991)

"The work in the mines is very hard. At the age of forty our miners are no longer potent," Nadya said with an embarrassed giggle. "Many women even refuse to marry miners for this reason." Lena asked about the work of women in mines. "They are so tired they don't want anything more," Nadya answered.

Nadya had joined the party in 1963, when she was twenty-three. For the next ten years she worked as a party clerk and followed the orders of the District Party Committee. "No one dared to question those orders, even if they were wrong," she said. "The only reason I gave up this work was because I wanted to earn more money so that my pension would be higher.

"During the last few years many members left the party but those are the ones who joined to make a career. They had different aims than I. I have no intention of leaving the party, even when people today accuse Communists of ruining the country. I will continue to try to build a better society."

Our hostess was typical of many Communists who never criticized a party decision and believed every word of the party leadership. She praised the system of rationing, which made scarce products available. For example, her family of three was now entitled to buy six bottles of vodka per month. Before they were lucky if they could buy one. In addition, each person was allotted 400 grams of oil and 300 grams of butter.

"I could live without sausage and meat. I am only afraid of war," Nadya said. I pointed out that the danger of war hardly existed today. Hunger was now a serious threat to the Soviet Union. "We have always had shortages, but I am not worried. We have a garage in which we store canned vegetables, potatoes, cabbage, and salted meat. Everyone has such rations. This year we have less than in previous years, but I think the situation is not that bad." "How long will your rations last?" I asked. "Several months," she said, and then I let Lena return to her favorite subject—party dues.

Lena strenuously objected to the fee Communist party members have to pay to the party and said to Nadya, "Do you know that your party fees enrich party officials?" Nadya's usual response to unpleasant questions was to put another portion of potatoes, herring, or tomatoes on our plates or to suggest that we drink a toast. This time she said, "I know that our fees are spent to help those who fought in Afghanistan." She had belonged to a party commission that dealt with the housing conditions of the workers and said authoritatively that workers in one mine were building housing for veterans of the Afghanistan war.

Lena praised Nadya for participating in activities that helped others, but reminded her that the party was responsible for the low living standard in the country. "If the primary aim of the system is the welfare of the people, the wages should be higher and people should be able to buy something with their money. If we had more parties in our country the rights of the people would be protected," Lena said. Nadya began, "The party is the only stabilizing influence in the country, and although it has made mistakes, I think ..." Lena interrupted the unperturbed Nadya to say, "You are a product of this system. When you are told to do something, you do it without asking questions or voicing doubts. You are a slave." To soften her attack, Lena complimented Nadya's smooth skin, which was free of wrinkles, and Nadya smiled happily.

The following day we met Nadya's husband, and he revealed the difficulties his wife's party membership had created for him. The party bosses wanted to know why his wife was a Communist and he, who was a foreman in a mine, was not. "I have always said what I think and know this is not possible as a party member. My wife believes in a firm party hand, whereas my twenty-one-year-old daughter and I believe in strong people's power. I think that the president is entitled to wield his power only when he is elected by the people."

A visit to a mine was not on our program, but after I insisted and bureaucratic questions were settled, my request was granted. Later I understood why special permission was required for this visit and why the miners tried to discourage me from undertaking this venture, which began quite harmlessly.

A "Glory to Miners" poster stood at the entrance to the driveway, which led to the administration building of the mine. It was necessary to walk through endless corridors of this building to reach the women's dressing room. Street attire was not worn in mines. Our escort instructed us to strip down to our underwear and put on miner's attire; but first she had to find my size, which was not easy. Not many women miners are 178 centimeters tall [5 feet 8 inches]. Finally she had success and handed me a pair of long, loose white underpants and a long-sleeved undershirt, which I was to wear under gray baggy pants and a jacket. Lena bound my feet in a piece of cotton material that was supposed to keep them warm inside the oversize galoshes. A belt, pulled very tight, kept my pants from falling down. To it was attached a battery for the flashlight that was affixed to my orange metal helmet. After putting on large, loose cotton gloves, we were ready for the trek from the administration building to the entrance to the mine.

A five-minute walk through the snow led us to a dark tunnel, which our weak batteries lit dimly. I was determined that the icy puddles, the penetrating cold, wet air, and the treacherous metal obstacles, which I repeatedly stumbled over, would not stop me, and I marched on with perseverance. From the pit head we walked down steep, wet, and slippery steps that seemed to have no end. Only my firm grip on the metal rail prevented me from falling.

We had to wait twenty minutes for the railroad car to take us to the next station, several hundred meters beneath the surface. This gave us a chance to talk to other miners who would soon begin their shift. Nadya's husband, who was our guide, said that the mine was built in 1940 and needed to be modernized. Most of the work was still being done manually. The system of ventilation and transportation was almost obsolete. When he was a foreman the workers received bonuses if there were no accidents. For the twenty-five years on the job he had received this bonus only three or four times. The miners in this mine had gone on strike for improved safety measures, he said. I gulped, but then comforted myself with the thought that this was probably the safest of all mines in Novokuznetsk. Otherwise we would not have received permission to be where we were.

Lena began talking to the young man sitting next to us, and I strained to hear what he was saying. He had been a miner for seven years and planned to quit mining in three years, when he would be entitled to a pension of 120 rubles. "I can earn big money for ten years and then change jobs," he said. The screeching noise of the oncoming train drowned out further conversation. We bent down to enter one of the low metal cars with room for six people in each compartment. For the next twenty minutes I held on tightly to Lena and to the side of the metal seat as we jolted and bounced along. The walls on either side were wet, and all kinds of objects jutted out. The dangers around me made me regret my decision to visit a mine, but it was too late to turn back. At the next station, we were supposed to walk down another hundred steep steps to the seam where the miners were working.

Before we began our last descent, a miner, who led the way, offered us part of his breakfast. If he did not finish it the rats would remove it from his jacket pocket, he said. When I heard the word "rat" I froze. Snakes and rats are the only animals I fear, and no one was going to force me to go one step farther. Suddenly I saw rats everywhere, although Lena reassured me that it was only my imagination. The miners laughed and tried to persuade me to change my mind, but it was hopeless. I had seen enough and, furthermore, could imagine what it was like in the seam where the miners were working in 100-degree temperatures.

The train that had brought us to this station had to reverse its direction and take us back. This time I no longer thought about the danger of the hanging pipes, the rickety and broken-down equipment, the exposed electric wires, or even about the number of miners who had been injured on the job or killed in explosions and floods during the past years. My only thought was rats.

To relieve us of a steep climb up the last several hundred steps to the entrance of the mine, the narrow coal conveyor belt was turned on, and we were told to lie down and hold on tight. Shortly before the end of the line, I was supposed to jump off the belt when I received a signal. My slow reaction almost cost my life. Two miners grabbed me and lifted me off the belt just before my head would have been crushed by a massive, low-hanging metal object. After this near-miss my legs were so shaky that I had difficulty putting one foot in front of the other. As I headed toward the sunlight and gray air I no longer thought about environmental pollution.

After recovering from our visit to the mine, I asked if it would be possible to visit an average miner's family. This time our wish was fulfilled. Alexei had the day off and he and his wife greeted us in their one-room flat, which they shared with their two teenage children. I immediately admired the ingenious division of the 18 square meters, which had a separate sleeping and sitting area. They had even found space for a piano and a large, old-fashioned sewing machine, which was operated with a pedal.

The walls were covered with a carpet, hanging shelves, and even a guitar, and the windowsill was wide enough for a television set and a desert of cactus plants.

My host was not accustomed to giving interviews to foreigners, and he appeared very uneasy at first. When he talked he moved his knee back and forth and twirled his thumbs in his clasped hands. It was difficult to establish a rapport during the short visit, and so we decided to let him speak and interrupted only when something was unclear.

His family shared the plight of 50,000 other families in Novokuznetsk, who had been waiting for a larger flat for more than fifteen years. Since the construction of new housing is a low priority in Novokuznetsk, living conditions have deteriorated for the miners but not for city, party, and ministry officials, he said. When an apartment is available they jump the line and take care of themselves and their kin. Alexei's director had just moved from a three-room apartment into a spacious four-room flat with his wife and two children.

Alexei's living quarters were much better than those of many of his fellow workers, who have been "camping out" for more than a decade in dormitories. I visited a few of these run-down, squalid shelters and was shocked that anyone was permitted to occupy them. The roofs looked as though they were about to collapse. Families of four lived together in a single, drafty room with only a hot plate for cooking. In some cases, fifteen families had to share a shower and toilet, and others did not even have hot water. The only conveniences they could rely on were cold water and electricity. Many dreamed of building modest homes for themselves, but construction material was in short supply, and they did not belong to the privileged class who had access to such precious goods.

"A miner has to die in an accident at work in order to improve his family's living conditions," Alexei said. After his death the family receives a certificate on which is written, "To the family of those who perished in an accident." This entitles them to larger living quarters, financial compensation, and difficult-to-obtain products, such as a color television or a refrigerator.

When I told Alexei about my experience in the mine, he said, "I risk my life every day I go to work." Unofficial statistics estimate that the average life expectancy of a miner is forty-eight years, which means that most miners do not live until their pension age of fifty. The difficult working conditions permit women to retire five years earlier.

"Safety measures are not a priority," Alexei said. A report I had read in the *Komsomolskaya pravda* confirmed this statement. In 1988, 152 miners died in accidents in the Kuzbass, and in 1989, 800 died in the entire country. Over the past ten years 10,000 miners died on the job. "That was a little less than the total number of losses in Afghanistan," *Der Speigel* reported (July 24, 1989), while the *Economist* reported that this was about 18 times as many as in America. (October 13, 1990)

"I am lucky that I have had only two accidents until now. Once I broke my leg and another time I broke all of my fingers because of defective equipment," Alexei said. "I must work twelve years more before I can retire. In spite of the danger, I do not have the qualifications to change my job. In this city one can be a metal worker, driver, builder, or miner. I come from a miner's family and have studied mining. Therefore I will remain a miner." Alexei belonged to the 50 percent of miners who have a higher education.

Alexei rose at 5 A.M. on workdays. By 5:45 he was on his way to the streetcar, which got him to the mine shortly after 7. He reached the pit at 9, and this is when the paid part of his seven-hour workday began. By 5 P.M. Alexei was in the mine's dressing room, where he had to share one shower with ten men. With luck he would be home by 6:30 P.M.

Alexei worked for three days in a row and then had two days off. At the end of the workday he said he was often too exhausted to play with his children, but when he had a free weekend they all went swimming. During his days off he often went shopping, such as the day before, when he spent four hours in line to buy sausage. He complained, like everyone else, about the empty shops and shortages of sugar, coffee, and tea, and we shocked him by saying that Novokuznetsk was better off than Moscow. "Then I have no reason to envy the Muscovites anymore. Ten years ago the shops in Moscow had everything and we had nothing. Young men would even fly to Moscow to buy their wives boots, which cost 250 rubles there and 1,000 rubles here." Now if his family needed shoes or clothing he went to the black market in Novokuznetsk, where the most expensive imported items in Siberia could be bought. With a monthly salary of 450 to 500 rubles, Alexei could not splurge often.

In spite of the high living costs he had been able to save 1,700 rubles, which he would spend on new furniture as soon as the stores finally had furniture. His dream was to spend his month-long summer vacation in a union sanitorium; but only one-third of the miners were offered this opportunity, and he had no connections.

In July 1989 he participated in the first miners' strike when the miners demanded economic improvements. The paltry result was a little more meat per week and a few rationed consumer goods, which were unjustly distributed. The authorities wanted to create rifts between the workers, and so they allotted one mine, for example, refrigerators or tape recorders—and another nothing. Two pairs of women's boots were allocated for 3,000 workers, two washing machines for 1,000 employees, four television sets for 1,200 people, and ten vacuum cleaners for 1,000 employees.

"The authorities claim we are independent, but how can a mine be independent when it has a debt of 4 million rubles? We don't even have money for soap and towels, which are small but important items for the miners. Our bosses drive Toyotas and Nissans bought with foreign-currency profits. They could just as well buy Volgas with rubles, and use the foreign currency to purchase urgently needed medicine for the miners and their families."

After the first strike Alexei decided to leave the party. This was at a time when one-third of the local Communists quit the party in Novokuznetsk. He had been a party member for ten years and said, "It is better to admit the bitter truth than to live with a lie. The party cheats and deceives its members, and gives them nothing in return for their dues." When he made this remark I glanced at Lena's nodding head and then at the picture of Lenin that stood in Alexei's bookcase. It was a good time to wind up the conversation, and we bid him farewell.

Alexei was like so many other miners who placed great hope in the future role of the working committee and the strength of the new independent trade union. After the first two strikes, the miners were much wiser. They no longer were grateful for trifling payoffs and stopped believing in the promises of the authorities. Most important, they lost their fear of party officials, who had told them in the past that their political demands would lead to a civil war and to tanks being called in. If they united with other workers they realized that they could be a strong political force.

In the spring of 1991, 300,000 of the 1.2 million miners in the country went on strike for two months. Work ceased at one-third of the 600 mines. The miners blamed the policies of the government for their miserable living and working conditions, and they demanded not only a raise in salary but also the resignation of the Soviet government.

This strike, unlike the others, threatened to paralyze the metal industry and the entire Soviet economy. The seriousness of the situation was reported in *Pravda*, which blamed the miners for the 93,000-ton shortage of raw iron in the automobile industry. It also published letters from readers who accused the miners of selfishness, risking lives, and playing politics. In spite of the government's threat to enforce martial law, the miners remained firm and won support from other groups. Workers in the metal, chemical, automobile, and machine construction industries joined the striking miners.

The government finally recognized that the miners could cripple one of the world's largest coal producers. Gorbachev met with a select group of miners, but it was too late. Miners in the Kuzbass Basin issued an appeal to all Soviet miners, saying, "Only total stoppage and a firm No from all miners can relieve our people of a government incapable of radical reform and save the nation from hunger and poverty." (*New York Times*, April 14, 1991)

Only through Yeltsin's intervention was the strike ended. In May 1991 he flew to the Kuznetsk coal basin, which is the second largest producer of coal in the Soviet Union—after Donetsk in Ukraine—to negotiate with the striking miners. During his talks he did not make an attempt, reportedly, to persuade the miners to abandon their strike. He insisted it was their decision alone.

His efforts resulted in the transfer of authority over the Siberian mines from the Soviet government to the Russian Republic. In the future the Russian Fuel and Energy Ministry would be accountable to the miners instead of a Soviet ministry. Yeltsin promised to give the mines economic autonomy and suggested that the system of quotas and deliveries set by the central authorities be eliminated. In the future the mines were to negotiate their own agreements with customers.

The miners' victory set two precedents in the country. It was the first time that workers succeeded in influencing a political decision of the government. At the same time control of a major industry was transferred from the central government to a republic. Yeltsin's wresting of economic and political power from the Kremlin was a significant step in the direction of sovereignty for his republic.

In June 1991 Boris Yeltsin enjoyed another success. He became the first democratically elected head of the Russian government in almost one thousand years. The results of the election were a clear indication that the majority in the Russian Republic rejected the Communist party as the leading force. Even Communists have lost faith in the party. In January 1990 the party had 19 million members; in July 1991 it had fewer than 15 million. The Soviet people are now ready for a multiparty system, which would include, among others, the Communist party.

The road to democracy will take decades. In my circle of friends I have had regular contact during the past twelve years with three generations who had been born into a system that has deprived them of individual liberties. Degradation and fear had often made them passive and helpless.

The victory in August 1991 of the democratic forces, whose hero is Boris Yeltsin, showed the world that thousands of young and middle-aged Russians were willing to fight, and even sacrifice their lives, to de-

[margin handwritten note: decentralization]

fend their rights. I know that the coming years will be hard, and it will be enormously difficult to replace chaos with order in the Soviet Union. Only when human dignity is respected, and individual rights are guaranteed, will people struggle and work for the democratic reforms that will benefit their children.

ONE YEAR AFTER
THE PUTSCH

*A*FTER THE unsuccessful putsch in August 1991 and then the abolition of the Communist party, many wishful Muscovites awaited a kind of utopia. If Yeltsin could accomplish these remarkable feats, then he could perform still other miracles, such as creating justice, prosperity, and freedom.

My Russian friends, who were more realistic, understood that a better life resulted from giving the people responsibility and an incentive to work. If they were their own bosses they would work harder. After months of lengthy and heated discussions, a law allowing privatization was finally passed in summer 1992. The next months would determine whether privatization could occur in an orderly and just way.

Before this law was passed Yeltsin's government used shock therapy, which stunned the consumers. At the beginning of 1992 prices were freed, while salaries and pensions, at first, remained unchanged. The cost of a monthly card for public transportation went from 6 to 120 rubles. This severe economic measure resulted in 90 percent of Muscovites, according to official statistics, living below the subsistence level.

One year has passed since the putsch and now it is evident who the first winners and losers are of the economic and political reforms. One of the losers is Maya, who belongs to the new class of poor. I met Maya in winter 1992, when I brought her a food package from Door to Door, a German humanitarian aid association for Russia, which I founded in 1989. She had worked as a translator and was now a pensioner. Her tears of gratitude were followed by a remark I have heard frequently during the past months from people belonging to her generation. "For forty years I worked hard and honestly for my country, and now a generous German family, instead of my own government, has remembered me."

Nelly and Maya, who were both seventy-eight, had led similar lives. They grew up in a country whose government provided its citizens with a stable life and security. It guaranteed them living quarters, jobs, free medical care, free education, and a wage or pension that would cover their basic needs. Law and order reigned and the people thought, "Nothing can happen to us." The exception were those who were willing to risk imprisonment and the loss of all guarantees by advocating human rights, democracy, and freedom of speech.

Today freedom of speech is taken for granted and Nelly expressed her despair about the developments during the past years. When Gorbachev promised that life would be better in two years, she like millions of others believed him. Now she feels betrayed. "He raised our expectations and hopes and then let us down," she said. "Yeltsin is different," she continued. "He didn't make promises, he acted courageously. When he made mistakes he admitted them, and this made us feel closer to him. He warned us that life would be more difficult during the coming years. But we, the builders of this country, who gave it our best years, did not expect that our last days would be a struggle to survive."

At present Nelly spends her entire pension for bread and other basic food staples for her daughter and her two teenage grandchildren with whom she lives. Meat and fruit are luxuries, and her daily concern is how she can prepare a vitamin-enriched diet for her grandchildren on her small pension and her daughter's low salary. Children's nutrition is a new worry of many parents, including even one of my close friends who is a pediatric surgeon and father of three children. "Almost no baby is born healthy today," he said, "and the prognosis for the future is grim."

Not only are food prices astronomical, and in some cases at least one hundred times more than they were only a few months ago, but medicine is available only through costly bribes. This means that Nelly can no longer afford the medicine she requires.

During the 1980s when Soviet television showed scenes of old people in New York rummaging through garbage, she was appalled at the brutality of a system that tolerated such conditions. She was proud that she lived in a country that took care of its people. Today she passes old people rummaging through garbage containers and beggars with wrinkled and shaking hands. Others stand for hours on the streets peddling anything from a dented can of string beans to a bunch of parsley in order to make ends meet. Every day is a struggle for Nelly because she is uncertain what tomorrow will bring. "I have lived my life in vain, and now I do not even have enough money for my burial."

Nelly still believes that Yeltsin is the only hope for Russia, but at the same time she condemns the new, so-called Democrats who surround him and also the other group of Democrats who run the Moscow city government. "They are no better than the old Communists," she said, a remark I had often heard. "They enjoy privileges like their predecessors and use this period of chaos to enrich themselves instead of passing laws that would improve our lives," she said.

Her skeptical commentary confirmed what I had personally experienced. Through an unpleasant encounter with a deputy from the Moscow city council I learned to be wary of those who profess democracy. I also know Russians who have sent their children abroad to study because the situation is so unstable at home. Some have opened bank accounts in the West to secure their money, which they believe is not safe in Russian banks, and still others have engaged in illegal business deals to guarantee their own future and that of their family.

Nelly's daughter, Lena, and Larissa ("Miss Perestroika") belong to the generation between forty and sixty years old who have difficulty adjusting to today's economic world. They grew up in a system in which collectivism was the working principle and individualism was taboo. "Initiative is punishable," was a Russian proverb my friends took seriously.

Both women had enjoyed job security for nearly twenty years and were confident, until recently, that they would keep their jobs at academic institutes until they were pensioned. Their salaries were low and pay raises rare, but they were satisfied with their work and knew that their pension would be enough to cover basic costs.

Today they and their colleagues are panicked about the possibility of losing their jobs. The death of the Union and collapse of the economy have forced many institutes and factories to close their doors or reduce their staffs. According to official statistics 1 million people are currently unemployed in Russia and this figure could increase to more than 4 million by autumn 1992. Unemployment insurance and compensation amount to so little that those laid off are forced to seek new work. This creates a crisis for many middle-aged people who are not psychologically prepared to go job-hunting or learn a new profession.

Two of my friends, who belong to the growing class of poor and needy university graduates, are washing floors, doing secretarial work, and giving English lessons occasionally to support their families. Not long ago a former university professor was the driver for Door to Door in Moscow.

Larissa was even willing to work for three months at her institute without pay in order to retain her job. A national cash shortage and also a reduced budget at her institute had created this situation. Now she is once again receiving her salary; in a resigned voice, she said, "A driver earns five times more than I do, but I am too old and tired to look for a better-paying job, and who needs someone my age? If I were only ten years younger, I would have the courage and strength to begin a new life and do something on my own."

Galya is in her mid-thirties, just the age Larissa would have liked to be, and she has taken advantage of the economic opportunities that are now available to young people with courage, initiative, and talent. She spoke for her generation when she said, "Our time has finally come. Now I have the chance to fulfill a ten-year-old dream."

I met Galya during the 1970s when she was a student of economics at Moscow State University. At that time she was hardworking and ambitious. When she completed her studies she was assigned a job in a government ministry, and within a few months I noticed a change in her. The enthusiasm with which she began work was short-lived, and she had become a frustrated and disappointed young woman without any hope. She complained that her job was senseless and boring. No one even bothered to read what she wrote or listen to her ideas. She could not get along with her superiors, who were old Communist bureaucrats with party connections instead of working qualifications. Galya deplored their indecisiveness and reluctance to make any decisions for fear that a wrong decision could jeopardize their privileges and job security. Eventually she, like others of her age, stopped fighting the system that had killed their working spirit, and she spent her working hours doing the minimum.

Today she is working for a foreign firm, while her university friends have set up their own businesses or are stockbrokers on the new Russian stock exchange. She loves the challenge of her job and the responsibility she has been given. Like her friends, she often works evenings and weekends and when they find time to meet privately they usually discuss their jobs and exchange business contacts.

Galya is proud of her earnings today, which permit her to buy the most fashionable clothing, "So I will look like a smart Western businesswoman," she said. When she was a government employee her monthly salary was hardly enough to feed her son. "If my parents had not supported me then, I don't know what I would have done." Today she earns three times more than her mother, who has been working for twenty-five years as a doctor at a walk-in clinic. "At least I am financially independent, and I can even assist my parents," she said.

Galya's son is almost as old as Kiril and belongs to the generation whose behavior reflects how free and fearless youth are today. During the 1991 putsch many young people stood at the barricades and were willing to sacrifice their lives for democracy while their frightened parents stayed at home. Today they scorn domestic politics, and their interest is focused on almost everything that comes from the West, from computers to fashions, pornography, and even narcotics. Young capitalists, who were black marketeers in 1990, sell Western goods on the sidewalks of Moscow and earn more in a day than their parents in several months. They know that hard and honest work have brought their parents and grandparents nothing more than a low standard of living. These unskilled youths live for today, with a dream of visiting the West, and they do not plan for tomorrow. At the same time they see that the new rich are mainly former Communist functionaries, new democrats, Mafia, and black marketeers who have earned their millions through illegal or shady deals. Honest young people with talent and drive also belong to this new class of millionaires, but they are still in the minority.

The future of the country is in the hands of a growing group of young people who recognize that if they have knowledge and skills and are industrious they can find challenging work, live well, and even run their own businesses. Kiril is one of the many who has become aware of this new possibility. He has just begun studying economics at the university and understands that he must be qualified to compete in the future job market. "Now I have goals for the future, and success depends on me," he said.

Kiril is almost nineteen and is optimistic while others have reasons to be disappointed and pessimistic. The Union no longer exists and many former Communists, pensioners, and members of the armed forces are in a shocked state about the most recent developments. Their country is no longer a world power and, even more humiliating, they are dependent on the West for support. Mothers worry about feeding their children every day, and the generation over forty is concerned about threatening unemployment. The former social guarantees and security the majority of people took for granted no longer exist.

For seventy-four years the Communist party ran down the country and exploited and neglected its people. The present instability, lawlessness, and chaos in the country are the results of Gorbachev's and Yeltsin's attempts to correct the mistakes of the past and pave the way toward democracy. This way will be long and full of potholes, and setbacks are likely. In the worst case, a civil war could take place, and then the extreme Russian nationalists, former Communists, and some members of the armed forces might impose their form of law and order on the country. Until now the revolution in Russia has been peaceful and my friends say, "The longer we have peace at home, the greater the chance we have to preserve it."

My friends, who have not yet given up, see hope for the future in the establishment of small businesses, which would relieve a part of the unemployment problem and contribute to the rebuilding of the country. At the same time a law must be passed that returns the land to the farmers and provides them with adequate loans to run their own farms and feed their people. If these measures are not successful in warding off an uprising from the hungry and dissatisfied masses, then I can only hope that my patient and long-suffering Russian friends are correct when they say, "A miracle will save us."

About the Book and Author

AN ENGAGING ACCOUNT of life in today's turbulent Russia, this book faithfully presents the richly contradictory views of Muscovites and rural Russians on their work, their families and communities, their government, and their daily lives. Lois Fisher skillfully interweaves anecdote, conversation, and observation to round out the picture of a society in turmoil. Not surprisingly, much of the discussion focuses on the currently most pressing social issues—the economy and economic policy, education, crime, and social welfare. Other highlights include profiles of Kuzbass miners and their families and of former Red Army soldiers waiting in Germany for demobilization.

Written by a veteran foreign correspondent in a lively style, this book will have special appeal for students and general readers. The original edition, published in autumn 1991 by Hoffmann und Campe Verlag as *Überleben in Rußland,* ranked for many weeks as a top nonfiction best-seller. This English edition includes additions and updates on the lives of many of the individuals first encountered in the Original edition.

LOIS FISHER has worked since the 1970s as a writer and a foreign correspondent in Bonn, Beijing, Cologne, and Moscow. She has lived in Russia and continues to travel there often to maintain her ties and her familiarity with the language. Prior to embarking on her career in journalism, she served in the Peace Corps and on the staff of President Johnson. She is the author also of *A Peking Diary, Nadezhda Means Hope, Alltag in Moskau* (German), and *Meine Armenischen Kinder* (German).